Nepal

Everything You Need to Know

Copyright © 2023 by Noah Gil-Smith.

All rights reserved. No part of this book may be reproduced, distributed, or transmitted in any form or by any means, including photocopying, recording, or other electronic or mechanical methods, without the prior written permission of the publisher, except in the case of brief quotations embodied in critical reviews and certain other noncommercial uses permitted by copyright law. This book was created with the assistance of Artificial Intelligence. The content presented in this book is for entertainment purposes only. It should not be considered as a substitute for professional advice or comprehensive research. Readers are encouraged to independently verify any information and consult relevant experts for specific matters. The author and publisher disclaim any liability or responsibility for any loss, injury, or inconvenience caused or alleged to be caused directly or indirectly by the information presented in this book.

Introduction to Nepal: Land of the Himalayas 6

Geography and Topography of Nepal 9

Nepal's Rich and Diverse History: Ancient to Modern 11

The Shaping of Nepal's Identity: A Historical Overview 13

The Birthplace of Buddha: Lumbini's Legacy 16

The Mauryan and Malla Dynasties: Early Nepali History 18

The Unification of Nepal: King Prithvi Narayan Shah 21

Nepal and the British Raj: The Anglo-Nepalese War 23

Nepal's Transition to Democracy: Recent Political History 26

Wildlife in Nepal: A Biodiversity Hotspot 28

Exploring Nepal's Varied Cuisine: From Momos to Dal Bhat 30

The Art of Thangka Painting: A Nepali Tradition 32

Ancient Architecture of Nepal: Pagodas and Stupas 35

The Kathmandu Valley: A Cultural Treasure Trove 38

Bhaktapur: The City of Devotees 41

Patan: The City of Fine Arts 43

Kathmandu: Nepal's Vibrant Capital 45

The Mystique of the Himalayas: Trekking in Nepal 48

Annapurna Circuit: A Trekker's Paradise 50

Everest Base Camp: A Legendary Expedition 52

Langtang Valley: Serenity in the Mountains 54

Chitwan National Park: Exploring the Jungle 56

Lush Greenery of Bardia National Park 58

Rara Lake: Nepal's Hidden Gem 60

Pokhara: Gateway to Adventure 62

The Cultural Significance of Hinduism in Nepal 65

Buddhism in Nepal: A Spiritual Journey 68

Shamanism and Indigenous Beliefs 71

Festivals of Nepal: Celebrating Diversity 74

The Living Goddess: Kumari of Kathmandu 77

The Traditional Dress of Nepal: Dhaka Topi and Gunyo Cholo 79

Music and Dance in Nepali Culture 81

Religion and Tolerance in Nepal 84

The Nepali Language: A Glimpse into Linguistic Diversity 87

The Nepali Language: A Glimpse into Linguistic Diversity 90

Writing Systems of Nepal: Devanagari and More 92

The Nepali Alphabet: Vowels and Consonants 95

Learning Nepali: Basic Phrases and Expressions 98

Nepali Etiquette and Customs 101

Handicrafts and Souvenirs: Bringing Nepal Home 104

The Influence of Tibetan Culture in Nepal 107

The Gurkhas: Nepal's Brave Warriors 109

The 2015 Earthquake and Nepal's Resilience 111

Nepal's Economic Landscape: Challenges and Opportunities 113

Sustainable Tourism in Nepal: Preserving Natural Beauty 116

Epilogue 119

Introduction to Nepal: Land of the Himalayas

Nestled in the heart of South Asia lies Nepal, a land of breathtaking beauty and profound cultural richness. This slender country, sandwiched between the giant neighbors of India and China, is often referred to as the "Land of the Himalayas." And indeed, it's an apt description, as Nepal boasts some of the world's most awe-inspiring mountain ranges, including the majestic Himalayas.

The very name "Himalaya" conjures up images of towering peaks, snowy summits, and dramatic landscapes. Nepal's geography is dominated by these formidable mountains, stretching across its northern border like a formidable natural fortress. Of these peaks, none is more famous than Mount Everest, the world's tallest mountain, reaching a staggering height of 29,032 feet (8,849 meters) above sea level. Its allure has drawn adventurers and mountaineers from across the globe, seeking to conquer the ultimate challenge.

Beyond Everest, Nepal is home to an impressive roster of other "eight-thousanders," mountains that exceed 8,000 meters in elevation. These include Kanchenjunga, Lhotse, and Makalu, each a testament to the geological forces that have shaped this region over millennia. The Himalayas, often referred to as the "Abode of Snow," not only dominate Nepal's northern skyline but also play a vital role in shaping its climate, culture, and way of life.

But Nepal is not just a land of towering peaks; it's a land of immense diversity. As you journey from the northern mountains toward the southern lowlands, you'll encounter an astounding range of ecosystems, from alpine meadows to lush subtropical jungles. Nepal's geographical diversity contributes to its remarkable biodiversity, making it a paradise for nature enthusiasts and wildlife lovers.

The country's intricate river systems, nourished by the Himalayan glaciers, carve their way through deep valleys, creating fertile plains where agriculture thrives. Nepal's landscape is a tapestry of lush terraced fields, vibrant forests, and tranquil lakes, all framed by the towering giants of the Himalayas.

Nepal's history is as rich and diverse as its landscape. Archaeological evidence suggests that humans have inhabited this region for thousands of years, with early civilizations flourishing along the fertile banks of the Kathmandu Valley. Over the centuries, Nepal has been a melting pot of cultures, shaped by the influences of India, Tibet, and other neighboring regions.

One of Nepal's most enduring legacies is its spiritual heritage. Hinduism and Buddhism are the two dominant religions, coexisting harmoniously and permeating every aspect of daily life. The country's numerous temples, stupas, and monasteries stand as testaments to the spiritual devotion of its people.

Nepal's culture is a vibrant mosaic of languages, traditions, and rituals, with each ethnic group contributing its unique colors to the tapestry of Nepali society. From the lively festivals that dot the calendar to the intricate art of Thangka painting, Nepal's cultural heritage is as diverse as it is captivating.

As we embark on this journey to explore Nepal, we will delve deeper into its history, culture, geography, and the experiences it offers to travelers. From the towering Himalayas to the bustling streets of Kathmandu, Nepal is a land of contrasts and complexities, a place where ancient traditions meet modern aspirations, and where nature's grandeur takes center stage. Join me as we unravel the mysteries and wonders of this remarkable nation, the "Land of the Himalayas."

Geography and Topography of Nepal

Nepal's geography is as diverse as it is captivating, offering a visual feast for the senses. Situated in the heart of South Asia, this landlocked nation is renowned for its dramatic topography, a product of the relentless tectonic forces that have shaped the region over millions of years.

To the north, Nepal is defined by its crown jewel—the Himalayan mountain range. These colossal peaks, known locally as the "Sagarmatha" range, boast some of the highest mountains on Earth. Towering above them all is Mount Everest, the world's tallest peak, which stands at an astounding 29,032 feet (8,849 meters) above sea level. This majestic mountain has captured the imagination of adventurers and climbers from across the globe, drawing them to its awe-inspiring heights.

But Mount Everest is just one star in the Himalayan constellation. Nepal is home to eight of the world's 14 highest peaks, all exceeding 8,000 meters in elevation. These towering giants include Lhotse, Makalu, and Kanchenjunga, each with its own unique challenges and allure for mountaineers.

The Himalayas not only provide an epic backdrop but also play a crucial role in shaping Nepal's climate. Their massive presence blocks the frigid northern winds, creating a rain shadow effect that results in the country's varied climatic zones. As you journey from the south to the north, you'll traverse a remarkable spectrum of ecosystems, from subtropical jungles with lush vegetation and diverse wildlife to arctic-like conditions at higher altitudes.

The southern region of Nepal is characterized by the low-lying Terai plains, which stretch along the border with India. Here, fertile land nurtured by the meandering rivers supports vibrant agriculture, and the Terai serves as a crucial economic and agricultural hub for the country.

Nepal's rivers are more than just conduits for trade and agriculture; they are also a source of natural beauty and adventure. The mighty Gandaki, Koshi, and Karnali rivers originate in the Himalayas, carving deep valleys and gorges as they make their way through the rugged terrain. White-water rafting and kayaking enthusiasts are drawn to these fast-flowing waters, seeking the adrenaline rush of navigating their tumultuous currents.

Throughout Nepal, you'll find a mosaic of landscapes, from serene lakes like Phewa in Pokhara to terraced fields that blanket the hillsides with vibrant green. These terraces, crafted over centuries, are a testament to the ingenuity of Nepali farmers, enabling agriculture to flourish in the challenging terrain.

As you explore the geography and topography of Nepal, you'll discover a land of stark contrasts and breathtaking beauty. It's a place where the towering Himalayas meet the fertile plains, where rugged terrain yields to peaceful valleys, and where nature's grandeur is on display at every turn. The geography of Nepal is not just a backdrop; it's an integral part of the country's identity, shaping its culture, traditions, and way of life. In the pages that follow, we will continue to uncover the many facets of this extraordinary nation, each one adding to the rich tapestry of Nepal's story.

Nepal's Rich and Diverse History: Ancient to Modern

Nepal's history is a fascinating tapestry of cultures, dynasties, and influences that have woven together to create a rich and diverse heritage. Stretching back thousands of years, Nepal's past is a testament to human resilience, creativity, and adaptability.

The origins of Nepal's history are shrouded in the mists of time, but archaeological evidence suggests that humans have inhabited this region for millennia. Ancient settlements have been discovered in the Kathmandu Valley, bearing witness to a civilization that thrived here as early as the 7th century BC. These early inhabitants cultivated the fertile land and developed their own unique culture.

One of the defining moments in Nepal's history was the arrival of the Kirats, an ancient Himalayan people, who are believed to have ruled the region from the 7th century BC to the 4th century AD. Their influence can still be seen in certain aspects of Nepali culture today.

In the centuries that followed, Nepal saw the rise and fall of several dynasties, including the Lichhavis and the Mallas. The Malla period, in particular, was marked by a flourishing of art, culture, and architecture. The Kathmandu Valley, with its intricate temples and palaces, bears witness to the Malla dynasty's enduring legacy.

The 18th century brought about a significant turning point in Nepal's history with the rise of King Prithvi Narayan

Shah. He embarked on a campaign of unification, gradually bringing together the diverse kingdoms and principalities that would become modern Nepal. His vision and military prowess culminated in the formation of a unified Nepal in the late 18th century.

The 19th century saw Nepal caught in the crosshairs of the British Empire. The Anglo-Nepalese War of 1814-1816, also known as the Gurkha War, resulted in the Treaty of Sugauli, which ceded significant territories to the British, shaping Nepal's modern borders.

Nepal's transition to a constitutional monarchy occurred in the mid-20th century, culminating in the overthrow of the Rana regime in 1951. The country's journey towards democracy was marked by political changes, including the adoption of a new constitution in 1959 and the establishment of a parliamentary system in 1990.

The early 21st century brought its own set of challenges and changes to Nepal's history. The monarchy was abolished in 2008, and Nepal officially became a federal democratic republic. The country has experienced periods of political turmoil and reconstruction, most notably after the devastating earthquake in 2015.

Nepal's history is a complex and multifaceted narrative, shaped by both internal dynamics and external influences. It is a testament to the resilience of its people, who have navigated through centuries of change while preserving their unique cultural heritage. As we delve deeper into Nepal's history, we will uncover the many layers of this remarkable story, from its ancient origins to its modern-day evolution.

The Shaping of Nepal's Identity: A Historical Overview

The shaping of Nepal's identity is an intricate journey through time, marked by a rich tapestry of cultures, traditions, and historical events. This landlocked nation, nestled amidst the towering peaks of the Himalayas, has a history that is as diverse as its landscapes.

Nepal's earliest inhabitants were likely the Kirats, an indigenous people who settled in the region around 7th century BC. Their legacy still lingers in the form of customs, language, and some cultural practices that have been passed down through generations. However, Nepal's identity was far from monolithic even in its early days, as various ethnic groups and communities coexisted and interacted.

One of the pivotal moments in Nepal's history was the arrival of Buddhism. This ancient religion took root in the Kathmandu Valley, leaving a profound impact on the region's culture and spirituality. Monasteries and stupas, such as the iconic Swayambhunath (also known as the Monkey Temple), became centers of Buddhist worship and learning.

As the centuries passed, Hinduism also gained prominence in Nepal. The melding of Buddhist and Hindu beliefs gave rise to a unique syncretic tradition known as "Nepalism." This harmonious coexistence of two major religions became a defining characteristic of Nepal's identity.

The Malla period, which lasted from the 12th to the 18th century, was a golden era for the Kathmandu Valley. During this time, the valley was divided into several small kingdoms ruled by the Malla kings. Their patronage of the arts and architecture left an indelible mark on the region, resulting in the exquisite temples, palaces, and artistic traditions that continue to define Nepal's cultural heritage.

In the late 18th century, King Prithvi Narayan Shah embarked on a campaign of unification, bringing together the disparate kingdoms and principalities into a unified Nepal. His vision for a cohesive nation laid the foundation for modern Nepal's identity.

The Gorkha dynasty, founded by Prithvi Narayan Shah, marked the beginning of Nepal's monarchy. Over the years, Nepal's monarchs played a crucial role in shaping the nation's identity, even as the country faced external challenges, such as the British East India Company's expansion.

The mid-20th century brought significant political changes to Nepal. The 1950s and 1960s saw a series of democratic movements and reforms that ultimately led to the overthrow of the autocratic Rana regime and the establishment of a constitutional monarchy. Nepal's identity evolved further as it embraced democratic principles and institutions.

In the 21st century, Nepal underwent a profound transformation, transitioning from a monarchy to a federal democratic republic in 2008. This shift reflected the aspirations of the Nepali people for a more inclusive and democratic nation.

Nepal's identity is a complex and ever-evolving mosaic, shaped by its ancient origins, religious diversity, cultural syncretism, and historical milestones. As we continue to explore the historical tapestry of Nepal, we gain a deeper appreciation for the enduring spirit of a nation that has navigated the currents of time while preserving its unique identity.

The Birthplace of Buddha: Lumbini's Legacy

Lumbini, often referred to as the "Birthplace of Buddha," is a hallowed pilgrimage site that holds profound significance in the spiritual and cultural heritage of Nepal and the broader Buddhist world.

Located in the southwestern part of Nepal, near the border with India, Lumbini is believed to be the place where Siddhartha Gautama, who would later become known as Buddha, was born in the 6th century BCE. This sacred spot is nestled within a serene and tranquil garden, a place where the gentle rustling of leaves and the songs of birds create an atmosphere of profound serenity.

The exact birthdate of Buddha remains a subject of scholarly debate, but it is traditionally celebrated on the full moon day in April or May as Buddha Jayanti, a day of immense religious significance for Buddhists around the world. Lumbini's legacy as the birthplace of Buddhism is deeply rooted in history and spirituality.

Lumbini's historical roots can be traced back to the time of Emperor Ashoka, who visited the site in the 3rd century BCE. He erected a pillar with an inscription that marked Lumbini as Buddha's birthplace. This Ashoka Pillar, with its ancient inscriptions, remains one of the most revered relics at the site.

The Maya Devi Temple, named after Buddha's mother, is another iconic structure at Lumbini. It is believed to be built on the very spot where Queen Maya gave birth to Siddhartha. Pilgrims and visitors from all corners of the globe come to this temple to offer their prayers and pay their respects to the Enlightened One.

Lumbini's legacy extends beyond its religious significance. It has been recognized as a **UNESCO World Heritage Site** since 1997, a testament to its cultural and historical importance. The site has undergone extensive restoration and development efforts to preserve its sanctity and make it more accessible to pilgrims and tourists.

The garden surrounding Lumbini is a lush and tranquil sanctuary, with sacred Bodhi trees, reflecting pools, and meditative spaces that invite contemplation and introspection. Visitors often walk in silent reverence, absorbing the spiritual energy that permeates this hallowed ground.

The legacy of Lumbini is not confined to Nepal alone. It has a profound impact on Buddhism's global community, serving as a beacon of enlightenment and a symbol of the Buddha's teachings. Buddhists from all traditions visit Lumbini to connect with the roots of their faith, seeking inspiration and guidance from the place where Siddhartha Gautama's journey to enlightenment began.

As we reflect on Lumbini's legacy, we are reminded of the enduring power of sacred places to transcend time and geography, uniting people from diverse backgrounds in their quest for spiritual growth and enlightenment. Lumbini stands as a testament to the profound impact of one individual's spiritual journey on the world and serves as an eternal reminder of the teachings of compassion, wisdom, and peace that continue to resonate across the ages.

The Mauryan and Malla Dynasties: Early Nepali History

The early history of Nepal is shrouded in the mists of time, with the rise and fall of dynasties leaving behind fragments of a complex and intriguing narrative. Two significant dynasties that played pivotal roles in shaping the region during antiquity were the Mauryan and Malla dynasties.

The Mauryan Dynasty, one of the most prominent empires in ancient India, had a profound influence on Nepal's early history. It was Chandragupta Maurya, the founder of the Mauryan Empire, who first expanded the empire's borders into the northern reaches of the Indian subcontinent, which included parts of present-day Nepal. His grandson, Ashoka the Great, is especially renowned for his impact on the region.

Ashoka, after his conversion to Buddhism following the Kalinga War, became a patron of the Buddhist faith. His inscriptions, etched on stone pillars and rocks throughout the empire, included some that extended into Nepal. These inscriptions, known as the Ashokan Edicts, conveyed Buddhist principles and moral values, promoting non-violence and religious tolerance. They are regarded as early historical evidence of Buddhism's presence in Nepal.

During the Mauryan era, Buddhism began to take root in Nepal, influencing the religious and cultural landscape of the region. Lumbini, the birthplace of Buddha, is believed to have gained prominence during this period, with the construction of the Ashoka Pillar marking it as a significant pilgrimage site.

As the Mauryan Empire waned, Nepal saw the emergence of local rulers and chieftains. This transition period eventually led to the rise of the Malla Dynasty in the Kathmandu Valley around the 12th century. The Malla rulers divided the valley into several small kingdoms, each with its own king, fostering a dynamic and vibrant cultural environment.

The Malla period is renowned for its artistic achievements, with the construction of intricate temples, palaces, and sculptures that continue to captivate visitors today. The architectural marvels of the Kathmandu Valley, including the Durbar Squares of Kathmandu, Patan, and Bhaktapur, stand as a testament to the creativity and craftsmanship of this era.

It was also during the Malla period that the valley's cities flourished as centers of commerce, culture, and spirituality. Trade routes crisscrossed the region, connecting it to Tibet, India, and beyond. The exchange of ideas, art, and culture enriched the valley's heritage and contributed to its distinct identity.

While the Mauryan and Malla dynasties represent different epochs in Nepal's early history, they share a common thread in their contributions to the region's religious and cultural development. The Mauryan Empire introduced Buddhism to Nepal, leaving a lasting impact on its spiritual landscape, while the Malla Dynasty nurtured a flourishing artistic and architectural legacy that continues to define the Kathmandu Valley.

As we delve into this early chapter of Nepali history, we gain insight into the forces and influences that laid the foundation for the diverse and vibrant culture that thrives in Nepal today. It is a history marked by the ebb and flow of dynasties, the exchange of ideas, and the enduring legacy of a region that has always been at the crossroads of South Asia's rich tapestry of civilizations.

The Unification of Nepal: King Prithvi Narayan Shah

The Unification of Nepal under the visionary leadership of King Prithvi Narayan Shah stands as a pivotal chapter in the nation's history. This remarkable achievement reshaped the political and territorial landscape of the region, leading to the formation of a unified and cohesive Nepal in the late 18th century.

Prithvi Narayan Shah, born in 1723 in the Gorkha Kingdom, ascended to the throne in 1743. His reign would be marked by an ambitious vision: the unification of the fragmented territories that constituted Nepal at the time. Nepal was a patchwork of small principalities, each with its own rulers and allegiances, making it a politically fragmented and vulnerable region.

Recognizing the strategic importance of a unified Nepal in the face of external threats, Prithvi Narayan Shah set out to achieve his goal. His military campaigns were relentless and strategically planned. He first focused on consolidating his power within the Gorkha Kingdom, which he accomplished through a combination of diplomacy and force.

Prithvi Narayan Shah's military campaigns were marked by both tactical prowess and innovative strategies. His forces employed guerrilla warfare tactics, which were highly effective in the difficult terrain of the Himalayan foothills. Over time, his armies expanded their control over neighboring principalities and regions.

One of the key moments in this unification process was the conquest of the Kathmandu Valley. In 1769, Prithvi Narayan Shah's forces successfully captured Kathmandu, effectively bringing the valley and its rich cultural heritage under Gorkha rule. This event marked a significant turning point in the unification of Nepal.

Prithvi Narayan Shah's vision extended beyond military conquest. He recognized the importance of fostering a sense of unity among the diverse ethnic and cultural groups that inhabited the region. He promoted a sense of Nepali identity, encouraging the use of Nepali language and the adoption of common cultural practices.

The legacy of King Prithvi Narayan Shah is celebrated annually on the occasion of Prithvi Jayanti, his birth anniversary. His achievements laid the foundation for the modern nation of Nepal, shaping its borders and fostering a sense of national identity that endures to this day.

The unification of Nepal under Prithvi Narayan Shah's leadership brought stability and cohesion to a region that had long been divided. His vision, determination, and strategic brilliance transformed Nepal into a unified and independent nation, securing its future in the face of external challenges.

As we reflect on this historical chapter, we gain insight into the indomitable spirit of a leader who defied the odds and reshaped the destiny of a nation. The unification of Nepal under King Prithvi Narayan Shah serves as a testament to the power of vision and determination in shaping the course of history.

Nepal and the British Raj: The Anglo-Nepalese War

The Anglo-Nepalese War, a significant historical episode, serves as a testament to Nepal's resilience and its ability to defend its sovereignty against one of the world's most powerful colonial powers, the British East India Company.

In the early 19th century, Nepal was ruled by King Girvan Yuddha Bikram Shah, commonly known as King Rajendra. The British East India Company, under the leadership of Governor-General Lord Hastings, sought to expand its dominion in South Asia. The British were especially keen on gaining control of the fertile Terai region, which lay to the south of Nepal and offered valuable agricultural resources.

Tensions between the British East India Company and Nepal escalated due to territorial disputes and border issues. These tensions eventually culminated in the outbreak of the Anglo-Nepalese War in 1814. The war lasted for two years and would prove to be a formidable test of Nepal's military prowess and determination.

The British forces, armed with superior weaponry and resources, initially made advances into Nepali territory. However, the Nepalese Gurkha soldiers, renowned for their bravery and combat skills, presented a formidable resistance. The Gurkhas' fierce determination and the challenging terrain of the Himalayan foothills worked in their favor.

One of the most iconic episodes of the war was the Battle of Nalapani in 1814. Here, a small Gurkha garrison led by Captain Balbhadra Kunwar valiantly defended the Nalapani fort against a much larger British force. The Gurkhas' tenacity and skill in battle left a lasting impression on the British, who would later recruit Gurkha soldiers into their own army.

Despite initial setbacks, the British East India Company eventually gained the upper hand. A combination of attrition, diplomatic efforts, and the economic strain of the war forced Nepal to seek peace negotiations. The Treaty of Sugauli, signed in 1815, marked the end of the war.

The Treaty of Sugauli had significant implications for Nepal's territorial boundaries. It resulted in the loss of extensive territories in the Terai and the cession of regions such as Sikkim and parts of Garhwal to the British East India Company. Nepal also had to pay a substantial war indemnity.

The Anglo-Nepalese War, while a military defeat for Nepal, left an enduring legacy. The valor and reputation of Gurkha soldiers were so impressive that the British later began recruiting them into the British Indian Army, a tradition that continues to this day. Gurkhas have since gained renown for their service in various conflicts, including both World Wars.

The war also highlighted Nepal's determination to defend its sovereignty, even against a formidable adversary. It is a testament to the resilience and courage of the Nepali people, who, despite the loss of territory, maintained their independence and cultural identity.

As we reflect on the Anglo-Nepalese War, we gain insight into a pivotal moment in Nepal's history, where bravery and determination clashed with imperial ambitions. It is a chapter that continues to be celebrated in Nepal, honoring the enduring spirit of a nation that stood its ground in the face of overwhelming odds.

Nepal's Transition to Democracy: Recent Political History

Nepal's transition to democracy is a complex and multifaceted story that reflects the nation's enduring spirit and its people's aspirations for political change. In recent history, Nepal has experienced significant political shifts, moving from an absolute monarchy to a federal democratic republic.

The seeds of Nepal's democratic movement were sown in the early 20th century, but the transition to democracy gained momentum in the latter part of the century. The 1990 People's Movement, also known as the Jana Andolan, was a turning point. It was a pro-democracy movement that led to the restoration of multi-party democracy in Nepal after decades of absolute monarchy.

In 1991, Nepal held its first democratic elections, resulting in the formation of a multi-party government. This marked a significant shift in the nation's political landscape. However, the political scene remained tumultuous, characterized by frequent changes in government and power struggles between political parties.

The early 2000s witnessed a decade-long armed conflict between the government and the Communist Party of Nepal (Maoist). This conflict, known as the Nepalese Civil War, resulted in significant loss of life and widespread instability. It further fueled calls for political change and the abolition of the monarchy.

In 2006, following the signing of the Comprehensive Peace Agreement, Nepal took a historic step toward ending the armed conflict and embracing a new political era. The monarchy's power was curtailed, and the country moved toward a federal democratic republic.

The Constituent Assembly elections held in 2008 marked a significant milestone in Nepal's transition to democracy. The assembly was tasked with drafting a new constitution for the nation. In 2015, Nepal promulgated its new constitution, which established it as a federal democratic republic, further decentralizing power to provincial and local governments.

The transition to democracy in Nepal has not been without challenges. Political instability, ethnic tensions, and economic struggles have persisted. The nation has experienced changes in leadership and frequent political protests. However, the transition reflects the resilience of the Nepali people and their commitment to democratic values.

Nepal's journey toward democracy is ongoing, and the nation continues to grapple with the complexities of governance, social inclusion, and economic development. It remains a work in progress, but the determination of the people and their leaders to build a democratic and inclusive society underscores the significance of Nepal's recent political history.

Wildlife in Nepal: A Biodiversity Hotspot

Nepal, a land of soaring mountains and lush valleys, is not only renowned for its stunning landscapes but also for its incredible biodiversity. Nestled in the Himalayas, this small South Asian nation is a true wildlife haven, boasting an astonishing variety of species that call its diverse ecosystems home.

The Himalayan range itself is a vital part of Nepal's biodiversity. It serves as a natural barrier, isolating different species and giving rise to unique and specialized flora and fauna. In the higher altitudes, where the mountains are capped with eternal snow, elusive creatures like the snow leopard and the red panda roam.

Descending to the lower elevations, Nepal's lush forests come alive with an abundance of life. The country's national parks and protected areas, such as Chitwan National Park and Bardia National Park, are veritable treasure troves of wildlife. Here, you can encounter the regal Bengal tiger, one of the world's most iconic big cats. With conservation efforts in place, these parks provide a sanctuary for these magnificent creatures.

Nepal's jungles are also home to the one-horned Indian rhinoceros, a species that was once on the brink of extinction but has made a remarkable recovery due to concerted conservation efforts. These gentle giants can be observed grazing along the grasslands and riverbanks of Nepal's national parks. The country's avian diversity is equally impressive. Nepal is a birdwatcher's paradise, with over 870 species of birds recorded. Rare and colorful species like the

Himalayan monal pheasant, the national bird of Nepal, and the elusive spiny babbler can be spotted in its forests. Nepal's rivers and wetlands are teeming with life as well. The critically endangered Gharial, a unique species of crocodile with a long, slender snout, inhabits its waters. The mighty rivers are also home to various species of fish, including the iconic golden mahseer.

Venturing into the skies, Nepal's skies are patrolled by raptors such as the Lammergeier and the Peregrine Falcon. The country's high-altitude lakes, including the serene Rara Lake and Phoksundo Lake, are inhabited by cold-water species like the snow trout. Nepal's rich biodiversity extends beyond its charismatic megafauna and avian wonders. Its forests are a treasure trove of plant species, including medicinal herbs and aromatic plants that have been used for generations by indigenous communities.

This biodiversity hotspot isn't just about species count; it's about the intricate web of life that exists within its borders. It's about the harmony between people and nature, as many communities in Nepal practice sustainable living and coexist with the wildlife that surrounds them.

In recent years, conservation efforts in Nepal have gained momentum, with a focus on protecting and preserving its unique ecosystems and the species that inhabit them. These efforts are not only vital for the nation's own heritage but contribute to global biodiversity conservation as well.

Nepal's wildlife is a testament to the importance of preserving natural habitats and coexisting with the creatures that share our planet. It's a reminder of the fragile beauty of our world and the responsibility we hold in safeguarding it for future generations.

Exploring Nepal's Varied Cuisine: From Momos to Dal Bhat

Nepal's cuisine is as diverse and varied as its landscape, reflecting a rich tapestry of flavors and culinary traditions. From the bustling streets of Kathmandu to the remote villages nestled in the Himalayan foothills, every region of Nepal offers a unique gastronomic experience.

At the heart of Nepali cuisine is "dal bhat," a traditional meal that's a staple in almost every household. Dal bhat consists of steamed rice (bhat) served with a flavorful lentil soup (dal) and a variety of accompaniments. These can include vegetables, pickles, and often, a protein source like meat or fish. This hearty and balanced meal is not only delicious but also provides essential nutrition for the people of Nepal.

One of Nepal's most famous culinary exports is the humble yet irresistible "momo." These dumplings, typically filled with minced meat or vegetables, are wrapped in a thin dough and steamed or fried to perfection. Momos are a beloved street food and can be found throughout Nepal. They're often served with a side of tangy tomato chutney, adding a burst of flavor to each bite.

Nepal's cuisine is also influenced by its neighboring countries, India and Tibet. The result is a delightful fusion of flavors and ingredients. For instance, "thukpa," a noodle soup with vegetables and meat, has Tibetan origins but has become a popular dish in Nepal, especially in the Himalayan regions.

Nepal's diverse topography means that ingredients can vary significantly from one region to another. In the Terai plains, you'll find rice, lentils, and a variety of tropical fruits. In the hills, maize, millet, and potatoes are common staples, while in the mountainous areas, barley and buckwheat are prevalent due to the harsher growing conditions.

Nepal's vibrant street food culture is a testament to its culinary diversity. Stalls and vendors offer a smorgasbord of snacks, from "sel roti," a crispy rice doughnut, to "yomari," a sweet steamed dumpling filled with jaggery and sesame seeds. Food markets and bazaars are a sensory delight, with the aroma of spices and the sizzle of street-side grills filling the air.

Spices are an integral part of Nepali cuisine, with each region having its own spice blends and signature dishes. The use of ginger, garlic, cumin, coriander, and turmeric adds depth and complexity to Nepali dishes. The result is a harmonious balance of flavors, with dishes ranging from mild to fiery, catering to a variety of palates.

Nepal's culinary heritage extends to its beverages as well. "Chiya," a spiced tea, is a daily ritual for many Nepalis. It's brewed with a mixture of black tea leaves, milk, and an array of spices like cinnamon, cardamom, and cloves. The result is a comforting and aromatic beverage enjoyed throughout the country.

As you explore Nepal's varied cuisine, you'll embark on a culinary journey that mirrors the nation's cultural diversity and geographic contrasts. Each dish tells a story, connecting you to the land, the people, and the traditions that make Nepal's food so extraordinary. Whether you're savoring a steaming bowl of dal bhat, biting into a savory momo, or sipping on a fragrant cup of chiya, you're not just tasting food; you're tasting the heart and soul of Nepal.

The Art of Thangka Painting: A Nepali Tradition

The art of Thangka painting, a cherished and intricate tradition in Nepal, serves as a visual gateway into the rich tapestry of Nepali culture and spirituality. These exquisite scroll paintings are not merely artistic creations but also powerful tools for meditation and religious devotion.

Thangkas are traditional Tibetan and Nepali paintings that date back centuries. The word "Thangka" itself translates to "something that one can roll up." This art form is characterized by its vivid colors, intricate details, and religious motifs, often depicting deities, mandalas, and sacred symbols.

Nepal's connection to Thangka painting is deeply intertwined with its Buddhist and Hindu heritage. These paintings serve as a means of transmitting spiritual teachings and stories to the faithful. They are not static artworks but rather dynamic aids for meditation and contemplation.

The creation of a Thangka is a painstaking process that demands exceptional skill and patience. The canvas is typically made from cotton or silk and is meticulously prepared with layers of glue to create a smooth surface. The artist then sketches the design using precise measurements and proportions, ensuring accuracy in the portrayal of sacred figures and symbols.

Color plays a crucial role in Thangka painting. Artists use natural pigments made from minerals, stones, and plants, resulting in a vibrant and long-lasting palette. The application of color is a delicate process, with each hue symbolizing different aspects of spirituality and divinity.

One of the distinctive features of Thangkas is their precise composition. The central figure, often a deity or enlightened being, is surrounded by a complex arrangement of symbols, geometric shapes, and secondary figures. These elements are not arbitrary; they are carefully chosen to convey specific teachings and concepts.

The artistic lineage of Thangka painting in Nepal is passed down through generations of skilled artists. Young apprentices learn from experienced masters, honing their techniques and understanding of the spiritual significance behind each stroke of the brush. This transmission of knowledge ensures the continuity and authenticity of the art form.

Thangkas are not merely decorative; they hold a sacred purpose in religious rituals and practices. They are used as aids in meditation, helping practitioners visualize and connect with the divine. Thangkas are also integral to rituals and ceremonies, where they are displayed in temples and monasteries during important religious events.

Nepal's Thangka tradition is not limited to Buddhism alone. Hinduism, the predominant religion in Nepal, also incorporates Thangka-like paintings in its worship practices. These paintings depict Hindu deities, mythological stories, and symbols, adding to the diversity and richness of the tradition.

As you explore the world of Thangka painting in Nepal, you enter a realm where art, spirituality, and culture converge. These intricate scroll paintings are not mere artifacts; they are a living expression of faith and devotion. They invite you to delve deeper into the profound spiritual heritage of Nepal, where every brushstroke carries the essence of a timeless tradition.

Ancient Architecture of Nepal: Pagodas and Stupas

The ancient architecture of Nepal, characterized by its distinctive pagodas and stupas, is a living testament to the rich cultural and religious heritage of this Himalayan nation. These architectural marvels have not only withstood the test of time but have also served as profound symbols of spirituality, artistry, and craftsmanship.

Pagodas, with their tiered roofs and ornate woodcarvings, are iconic structures in Nepal's architectural landscape. These elegant and towering temples have been a hallmark of Nepali architecture for centuries. The pagoda style is synonymous with Nepal's religious traditions, especially in Hinduism and Buddhism.

One of the most renowned pagoda-style temples in Nepal is the Pashupatinath Temple in Kathmandu. This sacred Hindu temple, dedicated to Lord Shiva, boasts intricate wooden carvings and a two-tiered pagoda roof adorned with gilded copper. Pashupatinath is not only a place of worship but also a UNESCO World Heritage Site and a center for religious and cultural activities.

Another architectural gem is the Nyatapola Temple in Bhaktapur, a masterpiece of pagoda architecture. Standing at five stories high, it is one of the tallest pagoda-style temples in Nepal. Its guardian figures, known as "dwarapalas," flank the entrance, while the temple's tiered roof is crowned with statues of goddesses. Nyatapola

Temple is a testament to the ingenuity of Nepali architects and artisans.

Stupas, on the other hand, are dome-shaped structures that have deep religious significance in Buddhism. They are not only places of worship but also monuments that represent the Buddha's teachings and the path to enlightenment. The Swayambhunath Stupa, often referred to as the "Monkey Temple" due to the resident macaque population, is one of Nepal's most iconic landmarks. Perched atop a hill in the Kathmandu Valley, this ancient stupa is adorned with the all-seeing eyes of Buddha and a golden spire.

The Boudhanath Stupa, another UNESCO World Heritage Site, is one of the largest stupas in Nepal and a focal point for Tibetan Buddhism. Its massive mandala and prayer flags fluttering in the breeze create an atmosphere of spirituality and serenity. Pilgrims and tourists alike circumambulate the stupa, spinning prayer wheels and offering their prayers and aspirations.

Nepal's ancient architectural heritage isn't confined to the Kathmandu Valley alone. The city of Patan, also known as Lalitpur, is home to a wealth of pagodas, stupas, and palaces. The Patan Durbar Square is a treasure trove of architectural wonders, including the Hiranya Varna Mahavihar, a golden Buddhist monastery.

The construction of these pagodas and stupas relies heavily on timber and intricately carved woodwork. Skilled artisans painstakingly craft the ornate details that adorn these structures. The use of wood, coupled with earthquake-resistant design principles, has allowed many of these buildings to endure for centuries, surviving the test of time and natural disasters.

Nepal's ancient architecture is more than just a testament to the skills of its builders; it's a manifestation of spiritual devotion and cultural pride. These pagodas and stupas continue to be living heritage sites, where rituals, festivals, and daily life are intertwined with their presence. They are windows into the soul of Nepal, reflecting the nation's deep connection with its history, religion, and artistic traditions.

The Kathmandu Valley: A Cultural Treasure Trove

The Kathmandu Valley, nestled in the heart of Nepal, is a cultural treasure trove that beckons travelers and scholars alike to explore its rich heritage. This small but historically and culturally significant region boasts an astonishing concentration of temples, palaces, stupas, and monuments, making it a living museum of Nepal's past and present.

At the core of the Kathmandu Valley's cultural wealth is its status as the historical and spiritual hub of Nepal. The valley is home to three of the nation's seven UNESCO World Heritage Sites, a testament to its enduring significance. These sites include the Kathmandu Durbar Square, Patan Durbar Square, and Bhaktapur Durbar Square, each showcasing centuries of artistic and architectural achievements.

The Kathmandu Durbar Square, also known as Basantapur Durbar Square, is a complex of palaces, courtyards, and temples that served as the royal palace for the Malla kings. It's a testament to the architectural prowess of the Newar people, with its intricately carved woodwork, ornate windows, and pagoda-style temples. The Hanuman Dhoka Durbar Square, a part of this complex, is especially renowned for its historical significance and artistic grandeur.

Patan Durbar Square, located in the city of Patan (Lalitpur), offers a glimpse into the ancient kingdom of Patan. This square is adorned with palaces, temples, and a profusion of artistry in stone, wood, and metal. The Hiranya Varna Mahavihar, known as the Golden Temple, is a captivating Buddhist monastery with a golden façade and intricate carvings.

Bhaktapur Durbar Square, situated in the city of Bhaktapur, is a preserved medieval city square. It exudes an old-world charm with its red-brick structures, pagoda-style temples, and the renowned 55-Window Palace. The Dattatreya Temple, one of the many architectural gems here, showcases exceptional woodwork and craftsmanship.

Beyond the durbar squares, the Kathmandu Valley boasts an array of stunning temples and stupas. The Pashupatinath Temple, dedicated to Lord Shiva, is not only a revered Hindu pilgrimage site but also a center for cultural and spiritual activities. The Swayambhunath Stupa, perched atop a hill, offers panoramic views of the valley and is a sacred site for both Buddhists and Hindus.

The Boudhanath Stupa, with its massive mandala and prayer flags, is a focal point for Tibetan Buddhism and a symbol of peace and harmony. Its presence in the valley signifies the coexistence of diverse religious traditions within the region.

The Kathmandu Valley's cultural heritage extends beyond its religious monuments. The valley is a vibrant center for traditional art, music, dance, and festivals. The Newars, the indigenous inhabitants of the valley, have preserved their unique culture through generations, reflected in their festivals, rituals, and craftsmanship.

Exploring the Kathmandu Valley is like embarking on a journey through time. It's a place where ancient traditions blend seamlessly with modern life, where sacred shrines stand alongside bustling marketplaces, and where the past continues to influence the present. The valley is a living testament to the enduring spirit of Nepal, a nation where culture, history, and spirituality are woven into the very fabric of daily life.

Bhaktapur: The City of Devotees

Bhaktapur, known as "The City of Devotees," is a jewel within the Kathmandu Valley of Nepal, offering a glimpse into a bygone era of art, culture, and devotion. This ancient city, with its well-preserved architectural marvels and centuries-old traditions, stands as a living testament to Nepal's rich heritage.

Bhaktapur's history dates back to the 12th century when it was founded as a Newar kingdom. The city flourished as a center of trade and culture, and its prosperity is evident in its stunning architecture and urban planning. The medieval layout of Bhaktapur, with its labyrinthine alleys, courtyards, and temples, has been meticulously preserved.

At the heart of Bhaktapur lies the Bhaktapur Durbar Square, a UNESCO World Heritage Site and the city's cultural nucleus. This square is a mesmerizing ensemble of palaces, temples, and statues, showcasing the artistic brilliance of the Newar people. The 55-Window Palace, a remarkable wooden structure, is a centerpiece of the square. Its intricately carved windows and doors are a testament to the craftsmanship of Bhaktapur's artisans.

The Vatsala Temple, dedicated to the goddess Vatsala, is another architectural gem within the square. Its exquisite stone carvings and intricate details are a testament to the city's devotion to art and spirituality. The Nyatapola Temple, a five-story pagoda, stands as a towering testament to Bhaktapur's architectural prowess. It's one of the tallest pagoda-style temples in Nepal. Bhaktapur's devotion to the divine is not limited to its architecture; it's woven into the fabric of daily life. The city is a vibrant hub of religious festivals and rituals. The Indra Jatra festival, celebrated with grand processions and masked dances, draws visitors from near and far. Bhaktapur's residents also celebrate the Bhairab Jatra, during which the fearsome deity Bhairab is honored with reverence and revelry.

The city's devotion extends to its culinary traditions as well. Bhaktapur is renowned for its delectable cuisine, including the famous "juju dhau" or King Curd, a sweet and creamy yogurt served in traditional clay pots. Street vendors offer mouthwatering snacks like "yomari," sweet steamed dumplings, and "khaja," a crispy fried treat.

Beyond its historic square, Bhaktapur's narrow streets lead to hidden treasures. The Pottery Square is where skilled potters create intricate pottery using traditional techniques passed down through generations. You can witness the pottery-making process and even try your hand at crafting your own pottery.

The city's devotion to art and craftsmanship is also evident in its thriving Thangka painting industry. Bhaktapur is home to numerous Thangka artists who create intricate scroll paintings with rich religious symbolism.

As you stroll through Bhaktapur's alleys and squares, you'll experience a profound sense of timelessness. The city's commitment to preserving its heritage is palpable, making it a unique destination where the past coexists harmoniously with the present. Bhaktapur, "The City of Devotees," invites travelers to immerse themselves in its cultural tapestry, where devotion to art, spirituality, and tradition continues to thrive.

Patan: The City of Fine Arts

Patan, often referred to as "The City of Fine Arts," is a cultural and artistic gem nestled within the Kathmandu Valley of Nepal. This ancient city, just a stone's throw away from Kathmandu, is a testament to the Newar people's exceptional craftsmanship and devotion to preserving their artistic heritage.

Patan's history traces back to the 3rd century BC, making it one of the oldest cities in the valley. It served as the capital of the Malla Kingdom for over five centuries, from the 14th to the 18th century, a period that witnessed an extraordinary flourishing of art and culture.

At the heart of Patan lies the Patan Durbar Square, a UNESCO World Heritage Site and the city's cultural nucleus. This square is a living canvas of Newar architecture, with intricately carved wooden windows, ornate temples, and beautifully crafted statues. The Krishna Mandir, dedicated to Lord Krishna, is a masterpiece of stone and woodwork. Its 21 pinnacles and detailed carvings are a testament to the city's artistic prowess.

The Hiranya Varna Mahavihar, commonly known as the Golden Temple, is another architectural marvel in Patan. This Buddhist monastery is adorned with a golden façade and intricate metalwork. The interior is a sanctuary of tranquility, where devotees and visitors can find solace amidst the gleaming golden ambience. One cannot talk about Patan without mentioning the city's dedication to traditional craftsmanship. The city is renowned for its metalwork, particularly the intricate and ornate copper and brass statues and sculptures. Skilled artisans in Patan continue to craft these works of art using techniques passed down through generations. Patan is also a hub for stone carving, where artisans chisel and sculpt intricate designs on temple facades, statues, and pillars. The city's dedication to preserving these age-old crafts is evident in the meticulous attention to detail in every piece of art.

Another defining feature of Patan is its vibrant street life. As you wander through the narrow alleyways, you'll come across street vendors selling traditional Newari snacks like "bara," "yomari," and "khaja." The bustling markets, with their colorful array of goods, offer a glimpse into the daily life and commerce of the city.

Patan's devotion to the arts extends to its numerous museums and galleries, where you can explore the city's history and artistic heritage in greater depth. The Patan Museum, in particular, is a treasure trove of Newar art, housing a remarkable collection of sculptures, paintings, and artifacts.

The city's religious festivals, including the Rato Machindranath Jatra and the vibrant New Year festival of "Nepal Sambat," showcase the harmonious blend of tradition, spirituality, and artistic expression in Patan.

Patan, "The City of Fine Arts," stands as a testament to the enduring legacy of the Newar people's artistic heritage. It's a place where artistry is not just a skill but a way of life, where the past coexists seamlessly with the present. This ancient city invites travelers to immerse themselves in its artistic tapestry, offering a glimpse into Nepal's rich cultural and historical heritage.

Kathmandu: Nepal's Vibrant Capital

Kathmandu, Nepal's vibrant capital, is a bustling metropolis that serves as the heart and soul of this Himalayan nation. Nestled in the Kathmandu Valley, this city is a captivating blend of ancient traditions, modernity, and cultural diversity.

The history of Kathmandu dates back over two thousand years, with its origins as a prosperous trade and transit hub along the Silk Road. It served as the crossroads for traders, pilgrims, and travelers from India, Tibet, and beyond. Over the centuries, it evolved into a melting pot of cultures, beliefs, and influences.

At the heart of Kathmandu lies the Kathmandu Durbar Square, another UNESCO World Heritage Site. This square is a living museum of art and architecture, with palaces, temples, and statues that span centuries of history. The Hanuman Dhoka Durbar Square, a part of this complex, serves as a testament to the city's historical significance and artistic grandeur.

The Kumari Ghar, or Kumari's residence, is a significant attraction within the Durbar Square. The Kumari, a young living goddess, resides here and makes occasional appearances to bless devotees. This living tradition is a unique aspect of Kathmandu's cultural heritage.

Kathmandu's spiritual tapestry is woven with threads of Hinduism and Buddhism. The Pashupatinath Temple, dedicated to Lord Shiva, is one of the holiest Hindu shrines in the world. Devotees flock here to pay their respects and perform rituals along the sacred Bagmati River.

The Swayambhunath Stupa, also known as the Monkey Temple, is a revered Buddhist site that stands atop a hill overlooking the city. Its all-seeing eyes of Buddha and a golden spire are iconic symbols of Kathmandu.

Boudhanath Stupa, another UNESCO World Heritage Site, is one of the largest stupas in Nepal and a focal point for Tibetan Buddhism. Its massive mandala and the fluttering prayer flags create an atmosphere of spirituality and serenity. Pilgrims and tourists alike circumambulate the stupa, spinning prayer wheels and offering their prayers and aspirations.

Kathmandu's streets are a bustling mosaic of life, where ancient traditions coexist with the rhythms of modernity. Street vendors offer a plethora of goods, from spices and handicrafts to street food like momos and sel roti. The city's markets and bazaars are sensory experiences, where the aroma of spices mingles with the vibrant colors of textiles.

The Thamel district is a vibrant hub for tourists, offering an array of accommodations, restaurants, and shops catering to travelers from around the world. It's a place where you can find everything from trekking gear to traditional handicrafts.

Kathmandu's cultural richness extends beyond its historical sites. It's a city where traditional music, dance, and festivals thrive. The Indra Jatra festival, with its grand processions and masked dances, is a highlight of the city's cultural calendar.

Kathmandu is not just a city; it's a living embodiment of Nepal's history, culture, and diversity. It's a place where the ancient and the contemporary intersect, where spirituality permeates daily life, and where every street corner holds a story. Exploring Kathmandu is a journey into the soul of Nepal, an invitation to experience the heart of this captivating nation.

The Mystique of the Himalayas: Trekking in Nepal

The Himalayas, that formidable mountain range that stretches across several countries in Asia, hold a unique allure for adventurers and trekkers from around the world. Within this majestic range, Nepal stands out as a premier destination for trekking, offering an unparalleled experience that combines breathtaking landscapes, cultural encounters, and physical challenge.

The mystique of the Himalayas, with their snow-capped peaks, rugged terrain, and remote villages, beckons trekkers to embark on journeys of a lifetime. Nepal's Himalayan trails cater to a spectrum of trekkers, from seasoned mountaineers to novice hikers seeking a taste of high-altitude adventure.

One of Nepal's most iconic trekking routes is the Everest Base Camp trek. This trail takes you through the heart of the Khumbu region, offering close encounters with the world's highest peak, Mount Everest. Along the way, you'll traverse suspension bridges, meander through rhododendron forests, and stay in teahouses in traditional Sherpa villages.

The Annapurna Circuit, another renowned trekking route, offers a diverse range of landscapes, from lush forests and terraced fields to arid high plateaus. The circuit circumnavigates the Annapurna Massif, providing trekkers with spectacular mountain views and cultural immersion in the Gurung and Thakali communities.

Nepal's trekking options are not limited to these iconic routes; there are treks to suit all levels of fitness and adventure. The

Langtang Valley trek takes you through pristine forests and traditional Tamang villages, while the Manaslu Circuit offers a quieter alternative with dramatic mountain scenery.

Trekking in Nepal isn't just about the stunning landscapes; it's also an opportunity to connect with the warm and hospitable people who call these remote regions home. Teahouse owners, guides, and porters often become lifelong friends, sharing their stories, culture, and traditions with trekkers.

The Nepali people's resilience and spirituality shine through in the mountains. Along the trails, you'll come across Buddhist monasteries, prayer flags, and chortens, all bearing witness to the intertwining of nature and spirituality in this high-altitude realm.

Trekking in Nepal is a physical challenge that rewards trekkers with a profound sense of accomplishment. Altitude sickness is a genuine concern at higher elevations, but with proper acclimatization and care, it's manageable. The journey to Nepal's high-altitude destinations is as much about self-discovery as it is about exploration.

The logistics of trekking in Nepal are well-organized. Trekkers can hire experienced guides and porters to assist them on their journeys, making the experience not only safer but also more culturally enriching.

The allure of the Himalayas, with their mystique and grandeur, is a siren call for adventurers and seekers of the extraordinary. Nepal's trekking trails offer an opportunity to venture into these majestic heights, where the air is thin, the scenery awe-inspiring, and the camaraderie among trekkers, guides, and locals is unforgettable. It's a journey that leaves an indelible mark on the soul, a testament to the mystique and magic of the Himalayas.

Annapurna Circuit: A Trekker's Paradise

The Annapurna Circuit, often dubbed a "Trekker's Paradise," is one of Nepal's most celebrated trekking routes, renowned for its breathtaking scenery, cultural diversity, and challenging yet rewarding experience. Nestled in the heart of the Annapurna Massif, this trail offers a remarkable journey through a landscape that transitions from lush forests to high-altitude desert.

Trekking the Annapurna Circuit typically begins in the town of Besi Sahar, where trekkers register their permits and set out on a journey that circumnavigates the Annapurna Massif. The trail leads through a series of picturesque villages, each with its unique charm and cultural significance.

One of the highlights of the Annapurna Circuit is the Marsyangdi River Valley. Trekkers cross suspension bridges and traverse terraced fields as they meander alongside the river, surrounded by the stunning backdrop of snow-capped peaks. The villages along this section, such as Jagat, Tal, and Chame, provide trekkers with a glimpse into the daily life of the local communities.

As the trail gains elevation, the landscape transforms. The lush forests of oak, rhododendron, and pine give way to arid terrain, creating a stark yet mesmerizing contrast. The village of Manang, perched at an altitude of over 3,500 meters, marks a significant acclimatization point on the journey.

From Manang, trekkers have the option to embark on side trips to Tilicho Lake, one of the highest lakes in the world, or visit the ancient Braga Monastery, where Tibetan Buddhist culture thrives. These detours offer a deeper immersion into the region's cultural and natural diversity.

The crossing of the Thorong La Pass, at an elevation of 5,416 meters (17,769 feet), is a defining moment of the Annapurna Circuit. The ascent to the pass is challenging, often accompanied by harsh weather conditions, but the sense of accomplishment upon reaching the summit and the panoramic views of the surrounding peaks, including Annapurna and Dhaulagiri, are unparalleled.

Descending from Thorong La, the trail leads through the Kali Gandaki Valley, known as the world's deepest gorge. This section offers a dramatic contrast to the high-altitude desert, as trekkers encounter lush vegetation, waterfalls, and traditional villages like Jomsom and Marpha.

The trek culminates in the pilgrimage town of Muktinath, where Hindu and Buddhist devotees come to pay their respects at the sacred temple and natural gas-flame that burns near the temple complex.

From Muktinath, trekkers can choose to continue the journey through the Lower Mustang region or descend to Jomsom and take a flight back to Pokhara, concluding their Annapurna Circuit adventure.

The Annapurna Circuit is not merely a trek; it's an odyssey through diverse landscapes, cultures, and altitudes. It's a journey that challenges the body, invigorates the spirit, and leaves trekkers with indelible memories of a trekker's paradise that is the Annapurna Circuit in Nepal.

Everest Base Camp: A Legendary Expedition

Everest Base Camp, the very name conjures up images of grandeur, adventure, and human determination. Situated in the shadow of the world's tallest peak, Mount Everest, this legendary expedition is a bucket-list endeavor for many, drawing trekkers and mountaineers from all corners of the globe.

The journey to Everest Base Camp typically begins with a flight from Kathmandu to Lukla, a tiny mountain airstrip. From Lukla, trekkers embark on a trail that winds its way through the picturesque Khumbu region, characterized by lush forests, rhododendron blooms, and charming Sherpa villages.

Namche Bazaar, often considered the gateway to the Everest region, is a bustling trading hub where trekkers acclimatize before continuing their ascent. It's a place where traditional meets modern, with local shops selling everything from yak wool blankets to hiking gear and espresso.

As trekkers venture higher, they pass through villages like Tengboche, home to an ancient Buddhist monastery with stunning mountain vistas. The spiritual resonance of these places, set against the backdrop of towering peaks, adds a unique dimension to the trek.

The real challenge of the Everest Base Camp trek lies in acclimatization and altitude. Trekkers ascend gradually, allowing their bodies to adapt to the thinning air. Altitude sickness is a genuine concern, and trekkers need to be aware of the symptoms and take precautions.

One of the highlights of the trek is reaching Everest Base Camp itself, located at an elevation of around 5,364 meters (17,598 feet). This is where climbers preparing for an Everest summit attempt set up their temporary home. While trekkers don't actually climb the summit from here, they get as close as possible and soak in the awe-inspiring views.

Kala Patthar, a nearby vantage point, offers some of the most iconic views of Mount Everest. It's a steep ascent, but the panorama of Everest and the surrounding peaks at sunrise is nothing short of spectacular.

The camaraderie among trekkers, guides, and porters during the Everest Base Camp expedition is remarkable. Shared challenges, breathtaking scenery, and the common goal of reaching Base Camp create a sense of unity and purpose.

The Everest region is also a treasure trove of biodiversity, with rare and elusive species like the snow leopard and red panda inhabiting its remote forests. The Sagarmatha National Park, a UNESCO World Heritage Site, protects this unique ecosystem.

As trekkers descend from Everest Base Camp, they carry with them a profound sense of accomplishment, having experienced the grandeur of the Himalayas up close. The Everest Base Camp trek is not just a physical journey; it's a spiritual and emotional one, where the mountains inspire and humble in equal measure.

This legendary expedition is a tribute to human resilience, the indomitable spirit of adventure, and the enduring allure of the world's tallest peak. It's an adventure that etches itself into the souls of those who undertake it, forever connecting them to the legendary heights of Mount Everest.

Langtang Valley: Serenity in the Mountains

Nestled in the heart of the Himalayas, the Langtang Valley offers trekkers a serene and enchanting escape into the mountains. Often referred to as the "Valley of Glaciers," Langtang is a hidden gem that combines natural beauty, cultural richness, and a sense of serenity that's hard to find elsewhere.

The journey to Langtang Valley typically begins with a drive from Kathmandu to Syabrubesi, a charming village that serves as the starting point for trekkers. As you set foot on the trail, you'll be greeted by the sound of the Langtang River, a constant companion on this adventure.

The Langtang Valley trek leads you through dense forests of rhododendron and bamboo, alive with the melodies of countless bird species. You'll also pass through quaint villages like Lama Hotel and Mundu, where you can witness the daily life of the Tamang people, the predominant ethnic group in the region.

One of the highlights of the Langtang Valley trek is Kyanjin Gompa, a picturesque village with a Tibetan influence. Here, you'll find a centuries-old monastery and yak pastures that lend an otherworldly charm to the surroundings.

The trek's culminating point is Tserko Ri, a viewpoint that offers panoramic vistas of the surrounding peaks, including Langtang Lirung, the highest mountain in the area. The sunrise from Tserko Ri is a breathtaking spectacle that leaves an indelible mark on the memory of trekkers.

The Langtang region is also known for its biodiversity, with the Langtang National Park preserving this pristine ecosystem. Trekkers might encounter wildlife like red pandas, Himalayan tahr, and various species of pheasants and butterflies as they make their way through the forested trails.

The Langtang Valley is not just a trek; it's a sanctuary of tranquility. The absence of crowds, the serene ambiance, and the majestic scenery make it a perfect destination for those seeking solace in the mountains. It's a place where you can immerse yourself in nature, listen to the whisper of the wind, and marvel at the timeless beauty of the Himalayas.

The hospitality of the Tamang people, their traditional practices, and their warm smiles add a cultural dimension to the trek. You can engage with the locals, savor their cuisine, and learn about their way of life, creating connections that go beyond the physical journey.

In the Langtang Valley, serenity is not just a concept; it's a tangible experience. It's a place where you can find solitude amidst the grandeur of nature, where the mountains echo with the song of the river, and where time seems to slow down. It's a hidden treasure in the Himalayas, an oasis of calm that leaves a lasting sense of peace in the hearts of those who venture into its embrace.

Chitwan National Park: Exploring the Jungle

Chitwan National Park, a verdant jewel in the heart of Nepal, beckons adventurers and nature enthusiasts with the promise of a jungle exploration like no other. Nestled in the subtropical lowlands of the Terai region, this national park is a biodiversity hotspot that offers a fascinating blend of wildlife, lush forests, and cultural encounters.

The journey to Chitwan typically begins with a scenic drive from Kathmandu or Pokhara, taking you from the foothills of the Himalayas to the tropical plains of the Terai. As you arrive at the park's entrance, you'll find yourself in a world teeming with exotic flora and fauna.

One of Chitwan's most iconic residents is the Bengal tiger, a majestic and elusive creature that roams these jungles. While spotting a tiger is a rare and thrilling experience, Chitwan is also home to a diverse array of wildlife, including one-horned rhinoceroses, elephants, leopards, and sloth bears.

A safari in Chitwan National Park is an adventure that unfolds both on land and in the water. Jeep safaris take you deep into the heart of the jungle, where you can track wildlife with experienced guides. Alternatively, a canoe ride along the Rapti River offers a unique perspective, with the chance to encounter crocodiles, waterfowl, and other aquatic species.

Birdwatchers will find Chitwan to be a paradise, with over 550 bird species recorded in the park. The vibrant plumage of kingfishers, the regal presence of eagles, and the graceful flight of storks create a symphony of avian life that captivates bird enthusiasts.

Chitwan National Park is also a stronghold for the indigenous Tharu people, who have lived harmoniously with the jungle for generations. A cultural village tour allows visitors to gain insights into the Tharu way of life, their traditions, and their unique practices, including their intricate mud-walled houses.

For those seeking a more immersive experience, Chitwan offers the opportunity to participate in elephant safaris. These gentle giants take you on a journey through the jungle, providing a vantage point to observe wildlife from a close but safe distance.

The conservation efforts in Chitwan are commendable, with the park's management working tirelessly to protect its inhabitants and their habitat. The success in rhino conservation, in particular, is a testament to the dedication of park authorities and conservation organizations.

Chitwan National Park isn't just a jungle; it's a living testament to the wonders of the natural world. It's a place where the call of the wild reverberates through the trees, where the rustle of leaves may conceal a hidden treasure, and where the symphony of nature plays out in every corner.

Exploring Chitwan is an opportunity to witness the beauty of the jungle and the harmony of life within it. It's a journey into the heart of the Terai, where adventure and serenity coexist in the embrace of the wilderness. Chitwan National Park is an invitation to explore, discover, and marvel at the splendor of the jungle.

Lush Greenery of Bardia National Park

Bardia National Park, a pristine wilderness in western Nepal, stands as a testament to nature's untamed beauty. While it may not be as famous as its counterparts in Nepal, Bardia offers an exceptional opportunity to immerse yourself in a lush, green paradise teeming with diverse flora and fauna.

Located in the Terai region, Bardia National Park shares a similar ecological setting with Chitwan but is less frequented by tourists, making it an ideal destination for those seeking a quieter and more intimate jungle experience.

The park covers an expansive area of 968 square kilometers, encompassing dense forests, grasslands, and the tranquil Karnali River. These diverse ecosystems create a haven for a wide range of wildlife, some of which are rare and endangered.

Bardia National Park is celebrated for its population of one-horned rhinoceroses, which have made a remarkable recovery here thanks to conservation efforts. While tracking these magnificent creatures through the tall grasses and forests, you'll also have the chance to spot elephants, wild boars, and various species of deer.

Tiger sightings, although less common than in some other parks, do occur, and Bardia's dense vegetation provides excellent camouflage for these elusive predators. Leopards, too, call Bardia home, often moving stealthily through the undergrowth. Birdwatchers will be enthralled by the avian diversity within the park, with over 400 species of birds recorded. Colorful kingfishers, stately storks, and majestic raptors are just a few of the feathered inhabitants that grace the skies and waterways of Bardia.

The park is crisscrossed by an intricate network of rivers, creating an oasis in the midst of the jungle. The Karnali River, with its gentle meanders and vibrant riverbanks, offers opportunities for boating and observing wildlife along its shores.

A unique feature of Bardia is the chance to go on a jungle walk, guided by experienced naturalists and park rangers. These walks provide an intimate connection with the environment, allowing you to explore the jungle at a slower pace and discover its hidden wonders.

The local Tharu communities have inhabited the area for centuries, and a visit to their villages offers insight into their traditional way of life. You can engage with the Tharu people, learn about their customs, and even participate in cultural programs.

Bardia National Park is not only a sanctuary for wildlife but also a place of tranquility and natural beauty. The park's lush greenery, pristine landscapes, and untouched wilderness create an environment where you can reconnect with nature and find solace in its embrace.

Visiting Bardia National Park is like stepping into a world where the vibrancy of life is on full display. It's a place where the chorus of the jungle echoes through the trees, where the rustle of leaves may reveal an elusive creature, and where the lush greenery envelops you in its serene embrace. Bardia is an invitation to explore, discover, and experience the untamed beauty of Nepal's western wilderness.

Rara Lake: Nepal's Hidden Gem

Nestled in the remote northwestern corner of Nepal lies Rara Lake, a hidden gem that enchants and captivates those who venture into its pristine surroundings. This high-altitude lake, ensconced within Rara National Park, is often referred to as the "Queen of Lakes" for its sheer beauty and the sense of wonder it evokes.

Rara Lake is the largest lake in Nepal, spanning an area of approximately 10.8 square kilometers at an altitude of about 2,990 meters (9,810 feet) above sea level. Its crystal-clear waters reflect the surrounding snow-capped peaks and dense coniferous forests, creating a mesmerizing tableau that feels almost surreal.

The journey to Rara Lake is an adventure in itself. It typically begins with a flight to Nepalgunj, followed by a scenic flight to the remote airstrip at Talcha Airport. From there, trekkers embark on a trek through lush forests and charming villages, with the anticipation of the lake's beauty fueling their steps.

Rara National Park, where the lake is nestled, is a sanctuary for diverse flora and fauna. The surrounding forests are home to Himalayan black bears, red pandas, musk deer, and a variety of bird species. It's a place where the call of the wild reverberates through the trees, where the rustle of leaves may conceal a hidden treasure.

The lake itself is a serene expanse of azure waters, surrounded by rolling hills and towering peaks. In the summer months, vibrant wildflowers dot the meadows along its shores, creating a riot of color against the verdant backdrop.

Rara Lake is a place of quiet contemplation and natural wonder. Visitors can take leisurely walks around the lake's perimeter, basking in the tranquility of its surroundings. The stillness of the lake mirrors the peace that permeates this remote corner of Nepal.

Camping by Rara Lake is a unique experience, allowing you to fall asleep under a canopy of stars and awaken to the soothing sound of nature. The absence of light pollution makes it an ideal spot for stargazing, and on clear nights, the Milky Way sprawls across the sky in all its splendor.

For those seeking a more active adventure, Rara Lake offers opportunities for boating and fishing. The calm waters are perfect for a rowboat excursion, allowing you to glide across the lake's mirrored surface and soak in the breathtaking views.

Rara Lake is a testament to the beauty and diversity of Nepal's landscapes. It's a hidden gem that rewards intrepid travelers with an unspoiled natural paradise, where the lushness of the forest meets the serenity of the lake. It's a place where time seems to stand still, and the wonders of nature take center stage.

In the heart of the remote Himalayan wilderness, Rara Lake beckons with its quiet majesty, inviting you to discover and savor Nepal's hidden gem, a place where nature's beauty is on full display, and the soul finds solace in its untouched splendor.

Pokhara: Gateway to Adventure

Nestled against the backdrop of the Annapurna and Machapuchare mountain ranges, Pokhara is a gateway to adventure that beckons travelers with its natural beauty and a myriad of outdoor activities. Often hailed as the adventure capital of Nepal, this enchanting city offers a thrilling escape into the heart of the Himalayas.

Located approximately 200 kilometers west of Kathmandu, Pokhara is easily accessible by a scenic drive or a short domestic flight. As you approach the city, the majestic peaks of the Annapurna range come into view, setting the stage for the adventures that lie ahead.

One of the most iconic features of Pokhara is Phewa Lake, a serene expanse of freshwater that mirrors the surrounding mountains. The lake is a hub for various activities, from leisurely boat rides to stand-up paddleboarding. Boating across Phewa Lake, with the towering Annapurna range in the background, is a quintessential Pokhara experience.

The Lakeside area of Pokhara, situated along the shores of Phewa Lake, is a vibrant and bustling hub filled with restaurants, cafes, and shops. It's the perfect place to unwind after a day of adventure, where you can savor delicious Nepali cuisine or international dishes while taking in the lake views.

Pokhara is the gateway to some of Nepal's most famous trekking routes. The Annapurna Circuit, Annapurna Base Camp, and the Gosaikunda Trek are just a few of the world-renowned trails that start or pass through this city.

Trekkers often use Pokhara as a base for acclimatization and preparation before setting off into the Himalayas.

For adventure seekers, paragliding is a thrilling way to experience the beauty of Pokhara from the sky. The city's unique geography, with the lake below and the mountains above, creates ideal conditions for paragliding. Soaring above the landscape, you'll be treated to breathtaking aerial views of Pokhara and the surrounding peaks.

Pokhara is also a center for white-water rafting and kayaking, with the Seti River offering exciting rapids amidst stunning scenery. Whether you're a seasoned rafter or a novice looking for an adrenaline rush, the rivers near Pokhara have something for everyone.

The World Peace Pagoda, perched on a hilltop overlooking Phewa Lake, is a symbol of tranquility and harmony. A short hike to this pagoda not only provides panoramic views but also a sense of serenity in the midst of Nepal's adventure capital.

The nearby Sarangkot Hill is renowned for its sunrise and sunset views. It's a place where the sky comes alive with vibrant hues, painting the Annapurna range with shades of gold and pink. Sarangkot is a photographer's dream and a must-visit spot for anyone seeking to capture the magic of the Himalayan dawn.

Pokhara's cultural richness is also on display in the International Mountain Museum, where exhibits detail the history and culture of the Himalayas. It's an educational stop that provides insights into the mountains you'll be exploring.

Pokhara is a city that seamlessly blends adventure with relaxation, where the thrill of the outdoors meets the tranquility of nature. It's a place where you can embark on epic treks, soar through the skies, or simply unwind by the lake. Pokhara is not just a destination; it's an adventure waiting to happen, a gateway to the heart of the Himalayas, and a place where every day brings a new opportunity to explore, discover, and be captivated by the wonders of Nepal.

The Cultural Significance of Hinduism in Nepal

The cultural tapestry of Nepal is intricately woven with the threads of Hinduism, a religion that has left an indelible mark on the nation's identity, traditions, and way of life. As one of the world's oldest religions, Hinduism has thrived in the valleys and mountains of Nepal for millennia, shaping the beliefs and practices of its people.

In Nepal, Hinduism is not just a religion; it's a way of life that permeates every facet of society. From the daily rituals of worship in homes and temples to the grand celebrations of festivals and ceremonies, Hinduism is an integral part of the Nepali cultural landscape.

The majority of Nepal's population, over 80%, adheres to Hinduism, making it the largest religious group in the country. The rest of the population consists of Buddhists, Muslims, and adherents of other faiths, contributing to Nepal's religious diversity.

Kathmandu Valley, the cultural heartland of Nepal, is home to numerous temples and shrines dedicated to Hindu deities. Pashupatinath Temple, a UNESCO World Heritage Site, is one of the holiest places for Hindus worldwide. It's dedicated to Lord Shiva, the supreme god of destruction and transformation, and attracts devotees and pilgrims from around the globe.

Another iconic temple in the valley is Swayambhunath, often referred to as the "Monkey Temple." This stupa, perched atop a hill, is sacred to both Hindus and Buddhists and is a symbol of harmony between the two religions. The view from the stupa offers a panoramic vista of the Kathmandu Valley.

Hinduism in Nepal is not monolithic; it encompasses a diverse range of beliefs and practices. The pantheon of Hindu deities is vast, with each deity representing different aspects of the divine. The goddess Durga, for example, is revered for her fierce protection, while Saraswati is the patron of knowledge and wisdom.

The religious calendar in Nepal is filled with festivals and celebrations. Dashain, the most significant Hindu festival, is a time of family gatherings, feasting, and the honoring of elders. Tihar, the festival of lights, is another cherished celebration that pays tribute to animals, including dogs, cows, and crows.

Nepal's temples and sacred sites are not just places of worship; they are architectural marvels that showcase intricate craftsmanship and centuries of devotion. Pagodas, stupas, and intricately carved wooden temples are found throughout the country, reflecting the rich artistic heritage of Nepal.

The caste system, although officially abolished in Nepal, still influences social dynamics and traditions. It is rooted in Hinduism's ancient social structure, dividing society into distinct groups. While the caste system has been challenged and efforts made toward social equality, its legacy endures in some aspects of Nepali society.

In the rural villages of Nepal, traditional rituals and practices rooted in Hinduism remain a vital part of daily life. From birth ceremonies to wedding rituals and funeral rites, these customs are steeped in religious significance and cultural heritage.

The Kumari, or living goddess, is a unique cultural and religious institution in Nepal. Selected from a young age, the Kumari is considered the earthly embodiment of the goddess Taleju and lives in the Kumari Ghar in Kathmandu Durbar Square. Her role is to bestow blessings and is an enduring symbol of Nepal's cultural and spiritual richness.

The Cultural Significance of Hinduism in Nepal goes far beyond religious beliefs; it encompasses art, architecture, festivals, and a way of life deeply intertwined with spirituality. Nepal's commitment to preserving its religious and cultural heritage is evident in the reverence shown to its temples, rituals, and traditions. Hinduism continues to shape the ethos of this remarkable nation, offering visitors and residents alike a profound insight into the spiritual heart of Nepal.

Buddhism in Nepal: A Spiritual Journey

Buddhism in Nepal is more than a religion; it's a profound spiritual journey deeply embedded in the nation's history and culture. As the birthplace of Siddhartha Gautama, who later became the Buddha, Nepal holds a unique and revered place in the hearts of Buddhists worldwide.

Siddhartha Gautama, born in Lumbini, a small town in Nepal, around 563 BCE, is the central figure in Buddhism. His quest for enlightenment and the subsequent teachings that emerged from his awakening have left an indelible mark on the spiritual landscape of Nepal and the world.

Lumbini, often referred to as the "Sacred Garden," is a pilgrimage site of utmost importance for Buddhists. It is here, amidst the tranquil gardens and monastic complexes, that Siddhartha Gautama took his first steps and delivered his first teachings. The Maya Devi Temple, dedicated to Siddhartha's mother, marks the exact spot where he is believed to have been born.

Nepal's rich Buddhist heritage extends beyond Lumbini. In the Kathmandu Valley, numerous monasteries, stupas, and shrines stand as testaments to the enduring legacy of Buddhism. Swayambhunath, also known as the "Monkey Temple," is one such iconic site. Perched atop a hill, it is adorned with the all-seeing eyes of the Buddha and is sacred to both Buddhists and Hindus.

Boudhanath Stupa, another UNESCO World Heritage Site, is a spiritual hub for Tibetan Buddhists in Nepal. This colossal stupa is a place of meditation and devotion, with pilgrims circumambulating it while spinning prayer wheels and chanting mantras.

The city of Patan, renowned for its artistic heritage, boasts the ancient Patan Durbar Square. Here, the Hiranya Varna Mahavihar, or Golden Temple, is an exquisite example of Newar Buddhist architecture. Its gilded façade and intricate woodwork are a testament to the craftsmanship of the region.

Buddhism in Nepal is not limited to its historical sites; it's a living tradition embraced by the diverse communities that call the country home. The Newars, an indigenous ethnic group in the Kathmandu Valley, have preserved their rich Buddhist culture through festivals, rituals, and artistic expressions.

Nepal's mountainous terrain is dotted with monasteries and hermitages, offering seekers of enlightenment secluded spaces for meditation and introspection. The solitude of these high-altitude retreats provides an ideal environment for practitioners to deepen their spiritual journey.

Tibetan Buddhism has also found a home in Nepal, with Tibetan refugees establishing settlements and monasteries. The Kopan Monastery and the nearby Pullahari Monastery are centers for the study and practice of Tibetan Buddhism, attracting seekers from around the world.

Buddhism in Nepal is not confined to any single school or sect; it encompasses a spectrum of traditions, from Theravada to Mahayana and Vajrayana. The diversity of

Buddhist practices and teachings coexists harmoniously within the country's spiritual landscape.

Pilgrims and travelers come to Nepal not only to visit sacred sites but also to embark on an inner journey. The serene surroundings, the ancient teachings, and the vibrant spiritual atmosphere create an environment conducive to introspection and personal growth.

Buddhism's enduring presence in Nepal is a testament to the profound impact of Siddhartha Gautama's enlightenment and his teachings on the human experience. It is a spiritual journey that transcends time, inviting all who seek wisdom and insight to explore the path that leads to inner peace and enlightenment. In Nepal, Buddhism is not just a religion; it's a living, breathing testament to the enduring quest for spiritual truth.

Shamanism and Indigenous Beliefs

Amidst the backdrop of Nepal's rich religious diversity, shamanism and indigenous beliefs occupy a unique and often less-explored niche. These ancient practices are deeply rooted in the cultural heritage of various ethnic groups that have inhabited Nepal's diverse landscapes for centuries.

Shamanism, in its essence, is a spiritual and healing practice that revolves around the belief in the interconnectedness of all living beings, nature, and the spirit world. It is not confined to a single religion but is rather a set of beliefs and practices that vary among different ethnic communities in Nepal.

Among the indigenous communities of Nepal, shamans, also known as "Jhankris," play a crucial role as spiritual healers, intermediaries between the physical and spiritual realms, and custodians of traditional knowledge. They are revered for their ability to communicate with spirits, diagnose illnesses, and perform rituals aimed at restoring balance and harmony.

The practices of shamans often involve trance-like states induced through rhythmic drumming, chanting, and the use of natural substances. In these altered states of consciousness, they connect with the spirit world to seek guidance, healing, and solutions to the challenges faced by individuals and communities.

Shamanic rituals in Nepal are diverse and can include offerings to appease spirits, ceremonies to heal the sick, or rites to protect against malevolent forces. These rituals are conducted in sacred spaces, often in the open air or within specially constructed shrines.

Nepal's indigenous beliefs and shamanic practices are closely intertwined with animism, the belief that natural elements, animals, and even objects possess spirits or souls. This animistic worldview is evident in rituals that honor the spirits of forests, rivers, mountains, and the ancestral spirits of the land.

The Gurungs, a prominent ethnic group in Nepal, are known for their deep-rooted shamanic traditions. They celebrate the "Ghatu" festival, during which shamans engage in elaborate rituals to summon ancestral spirits, seeking their blessings and guidance.

In the high Himalayan regions of Nepal, the Sherpas hold a unique blend of Buddhism and shamanism. They believe in "Lamas" as spiritual guides and also consult shamans for healing and protection against the challenges of life in the mountains.

While the influence of organized religions like Hinduism and Buddhism has expanded in Nepal, shamanism and indigenous beliefs continue to persist, often as parallel systems of spirituality. This coexistence reflects the country's commitment to preserving its diverse cultural heritage.

In recent years, there has been a resurgence of interest in shamanism and indigenous practices, driven by a growing awareness of the need to protect Nepal's unique cultural heritage. Organizations and individuals are working to document, preserve, and revitalize these traditions, recognizing their intrinsic value in maintaining the country's spiritual and cultural richness.

Shamanism and indigenous beliefs in Nepal are a testament to the profound connection between people and the natural world, the enduring power of ancestral wisdom, and the resilience of traditions that have withstood the test of time. In the midst of Nepal's spiritual tapestry, these ancient practices continue to inspire awe and respect, reminding us of the deep and enduring connections between humanity, nature, and the spirit world.

Festivals of Nepal: Celebrating Diversity

Nepal, with its rich tapestry of cultures and religions, is a land where festivals are celebrated with unmatched fervor and diversity. Each festival brings with it a unique blend of traditions, customs, and vibrant celebrations that showcase the depth of Nepal's cultural heritage.

Dashain, often referred to as the "Festival of Tika," is Nepal's most significant Hindu festival, celebrated with great enthusiasm. It extends over 15 days and revolves around the worship of the goddess Durga. Families come together to offer prayers, receive blessings, and partake in feasts. Elders apply tika (a mixture of yogurt, rice, and vermillion) on the foreheads of younger family members, symbolizing blessings and protection.

Tihar, also known as Deepawali or the "Festival of Lights," is a five-day Hindu festival that honors various animals. Each day is dedicated to a different animal, including crows, dogs, cows, and oxen, symbolizing the sacred bond between humans and animals. The final day, Bhai Tika, celebrates the unique bond between brothers and sisters.

Indra Jatra is a vibrant Newar festival celebrated in the heart of Kathmandu. It is marked by the erection of the lingo (a ceremonial pole) at Durbar Square. The living goddess Kumari makes her public appearance during this festival, and chariot processions fill the streets with music and dance.

Maghe Sankranti, also known as Makar Sankranti, marks the winter solstice and the beginning of longer daylight hours. Families celebrate by feasting on traditional dishes like sesame seeds, molasses, and yam, believed to provide warmth and energy during the cold winter months.

Losar, the Tibetan New Year, is celebrated with great pomp by the Tibetan community in Nepal. It marks the arrival of the Tibetan lunar new year and involves prayers, rituals, and colorful mask dances at monasteries like Boudhanath and Swayambhunath.

Holi, the festival of colors, is celebrated with exuberance across Nepal. People of all ages come together to smear each other with vibrant colored powders and water, symbolizing the triumph of good over evil and the arrival of spring.

Gai Jatra, or the "Cow Festival," is a unique Newar festival celebrated in the Kathmandu Valley. Families who have lost a loved one in the past year take part in a procession with a decorated cow, believed to guide the deceased to the afterlife. It's also a time for satire, humor, and social commentary.

Bisket Jatra, celebrated in the town of Bhaktapur, marks the Nepali New Year. It is known for the chariot procession featuring towering wooden chariots and the exciting "Yosin" pole pulling competition.

Teej, a festival celebrated by Hindu women, is a time for fasting and worship to seek the well-being and longevity of their husbands. Women dress in red, sing traditional songs, and dance during this vibrant celebration.

Buddha Jayanti, the birth anniversary of Lord Buddha, is celebrated at Buddhist shrines such as Lumbini, Swayambhunath, and Boudhanath. Devotees gather for prayers, meditation, and candlelight processions to honor the founder of Buddhism.

Nepal's festivals are not limited to a single religious or cultural group. They are a testament to the country's spirit of unity in diversity, where people from various backgrounds come together to celebrate and uphold their unique traditions. These festivals not only provide a window into Nepal's cultural mosaic but also offer visitors an opportunity to immerse themselves in the vibrant and joyous celebrations that define this enchanting nation.

The Living Goddess: Kumari of Kathmandu

Nestled in the heart of Kathmandu, amidst the bustling streets and ancient temples, resides a living embodiment of Nepal's rich cultural and spiritual heritage—the Kumari. She is a young prepubescent girl chosen from the Newar community, and she holds a revered position as the living goddess of Kathmandu Valley.

The tradition of the Kumari is centuries-old, dating back to the Malla dynasty, which ruled Nepal's Kathmandu Valley. The word "Kumari" itself means "young, unmarried girl" in Nepali, and the selection process for this extraordinary role is a meticulous and arduous one.

The Kumari is chosen based on specific criteria, including her physical attributes and astrological factors. She must possess unblemished skin, dark eyes, and hair, and she should not have shed blood, as it is believed that this purity allows her to channel the goddess Taleju, a form of the goddess Durga.

The Kumari lives in the Kumari Ghar, a traditional Newar building located in Kathmandu Durbar Square. Her home is an architectural gem adorned with intricate woodwork and ornate windows. The Kumari's residence is her sanctuary, and she rarely leaves it except for special ceremonial occasions.

One of the most anticipated events featuring the Kumari is the Kumari Jatra or Kumari Jatra Yatra, a grand procession during the Indra Jatra festival. During this procession, the Kumari is carried in a palanquin, and she blesses the crowds that gather to catch a glimpse of her. The Kumari's presence is believed to bring good fortune and protection to the city.

The Kumari is not a mere symbol; she plays a significant role in the spiritual life of the Kathmandu Valley. Devotees, pilgrims, and even dignitaries seek her blessings and guidance. Her mere glance is thought to have the power to ward off evil and bestow blessings upon those who visit her.

While the Kumari is venerated as a living goddess, her life is far from ordinary. She receives an education within the Kumari Ghar, where teachers visit her to provide lessons. Her daily routine includes rituals and ceremonies, and she adheres to strict codes of conduct that reflect her divine status.

One of the most poignant aspects of the Kumari tradition is that it comes with a predetermined tenure. When the Kumari reaches puberty or loses blood due to an injury or illness, she undergoes a farewell ceremony and returns to a regular life. The selection process then begins anew to identify the next Kumari.

The Kumari tradition in Nepal is a testament to the deep spiritual and cultural roots that run through the Kathmandu Valley. It reflects the enduring reverence for goddesses and the unique way in which Nepal intertwines the divine with the earthly. The Kumari, with her enigmatic presence, is a living bridge between the past and the present, a symbol of Nepal's timeless traditions and the spiritual heart of Kathmandu.

The Traditional Dress of Nepal: Dhaka Topi and Gunyo Cholo

In the vibrant tapestry of Nepal's cultural diversity, traditional attire plays a significant role in reflecting the country's rich heritage and history. Two iconic elements of Nepali traditional dress are the Dhaka Topi and Gunyo Cholo, each carrying its own unique story and symbolism.

Dhaka Topi:

The Dhaka Topi, often referred to as the Nepali cap, is a symbol of Nepali identity and pride. Its distinct design and patterns vary across regions, but it remains a common sight throughout the country. This cap is typically made from Dhaka fabric, a woven textile known for its intricate patterns and vibrant colors.

The Dhaka Topi carries a long history, dating back to the early 19th century. It gained prominence during the reign of King Prithvi Narayan Shah, the founder of modern Nepal, who encouraged its use as a symbol of national unity. Over time, it became an integral part of Nepali attire and is worn during special occasions, festivals, and cultural ceremonies.

Gunyo Cholo:

The Gunyo Cholo is a traditional Nepali dress for women that consists of a Gunyo (sari) and a Cholo (blouse). The Gunyo, typically six to nine yards long, is draped elegantly, while the Cholo varies in design and intricacy based on the wearer's regional and cultural background.

Much like the Dhaka Topi, the Gunyo Cholo is a reflection of Nepal's diverse ethnic groups and their unique traditions. The colors, patterns, and fabrics used in the Gunyo Cholo vary greatly, making it a dynamic representation of Nepali women's cultural heritage.

The Gunyo Cholo is not merely a garment; it carries with it a sense of identity, belonging, and celebration. Women often wear it during festivals, weddings, and other significant life events. The Cholo, in particular, may be adorned with elaborate embroidery and mirror work, showcasing the artistry and craftsmanship of Nepali women.

In a rapidly changing world, where modern clothing trends have made inroads into everyday life, the Dhaka Topi and Gunyo Cholo continue to be cherished symbols of tradition and cultural pride. They serve as a reminder of Nepal's deep-rooted heritage, connecting the past with the present.

For many Nepalis, wearing the Dhaka Topi and Gunyo Cholo is not just a matter of tradition but also a way of honoring their ancestors and preserving their cultural legacy. In the midst of globalization, these traditional garments stand as a testament to the enduring spirit of Nepal's diverse communities and their commitment to upholding their unique cultural identities.

Music and Dance in Nepali Culture

In the heart of Nepal's diverse culture lies a rich and vibrant tradition of music and dance that reflects the country's profound connection to its people, spirituality, and natural surroundings. Nepali music and dance are more than mere artistic expressions; they are integral components of daily life and celebrations, weaving together a tapestry of sounds and movements that have evolved over centuries.

Music in Nepali Culture:

Nepali music is as diverse as the country itself, with various ethnic groups contributing their unique styles and instruments. From the soul-stirring melodies of the Himalayan regions to the rhythmic beats of the Terai plains, music is a universal language that transcends linguistic boundaries.

Traditional Nepali music often features instruments like the madal (a hand drum), sarangi (a bowed string instrument), and bansuri (flute), all of which add depth and resonance to folk and classical compositions. The harmonium and tabla, introduced through cultural exchanges with India, have also found their place in Nepali music.

Among the most iconic forms of Nepali music is "Dohori," a traditional genre characterized by duet singing, where two individuals engage in spontaneous lyrical exchanges, often accompanied by folk instruments. Dohori songs touch upon various themes, including love, nature, and social issues, and are an essential part of Nepali gatherings and festivities.

Dance in Nepali Culture:

Nepali dance is a captivating art form that encompasses a wide range of styles and traditions. Folk dances, in particular, are deeply rooted in the daily lives of various ethnic communities, and they play a crucial role in celebrating festivals and life events.

One of the most renowned Nepali dances is the "Masked Dance" performed by the Newar community during the Indra Jatra festival. Dancers wear elaborate masks and costumes, enacting stories from mythology and history. The dance represents a blend of artistry and spirituality and is a visual spectacle that draws crowds from far and wide.

In the Terai region, the "Sarangi Dance" is a folk dance that combines graceful movements with the mesmerizing melodies of the sarangi. This dance is often performed during weddings and social gatherings, embodying the spirit of unity and celebration.

Religious and Ritualistic Dance:

Nepal's cultural landscape is also enriched by religious and ritualistic dances. Devotees perform dances in temples and shrines as offerings to deities. The "Kaura Dance," associated with the Tamang community, is performed during Losar (Tibetan New Year) and incorporates intricate footwork and drumming.

In the sacred town of Lumbini, the birthplace of Buddha, Buddhist monks perform "Mani Rimdu" dances, which are intricate and symbolic expressions of Buddhist teachings and spirituality. These dances are an integral part of the annual Mani Rimdu festival.

Modern and Contemporary Expressions:

While traditional music and dance continue to thrive in Nepal, the country has also embraced modern and contemporary forms. Pop, rock, and fusion music have gained popularity among the younger generation, and Nepali artists have made their mark on the international music scene.

Nepali dance has also evolved to include contemporary and Western styles, with dance academies and choreographers pushing the boundaries of creativity.

In the heart of Nepal, music and dance are not just art forms; they are living traditions that bridge the gap between the past and the present. They encapsulate the spirit of Nepal's diverse communities, their reverence for nature, and their profound devotion to spirituality. As these traditions continue to evolve, they remain a testament to the enduring power of culture and creativity in the Himalayan nation.

Religion and Tolerance in Nepal

Religion and tolerance are deeply intertwined in the diverse tapestry of Nepal's cultural and social fabric. This Himalayan nation, nestled between the towering peaks of the world's highest mountains, is a living testament to the coexistence of multiple religions and spiritual traditions.

Hinduism:

Hinduism is the largest religious tradition in Nepal, with the majority of the population identifying as Hindus. The country is home to numerous sacred sites and temples dedicated to various Hindu deities. Among the most renowned are the Pashupatinath Temple in Kathmandu, the sacred Bagmati River, and the Muktinath Temple in the Mustang region. Pilgrims from Nepal and beyond flock to these sites to pay their respects and seek spiritual solace.

Buddhism:

Buddhism has a deep-rooted presence in Nepal, particularly in the Kathmandu Valley and the northern regions bordering Tibet. Lumbini, the birthplace of Lord Buddha, is one of the most significant Buddhist pilgrimage sites globally. Monasteries and stupas, such as Swayambhunath (the Monkey Temple) and Boudhanath, are revered centers of worship and meditation for Buddhists. The peaceful coexistence of Hinduism and Buddhism in Nepal is a testament to the nation's religious harmony.

Indigenous Beliefs and Shamanism:

Nepal's religious landscape extends beyond the major world religions to encompass indigenous beliefs and shamanism. Various ethnic communities, like the Newars and Tamangs, practice their unique forms of animism, ancestor worship, and shamanistic rituals. These traditions emphasize the interconnectedness of nature and spirituality, with rituals often performed to appease spirits and maintain balance in the natural world.

Religious Tolerance:

Nepal's commitment to religious tolerance is enshrined in its constitution, which guarantees freedom of religion and the right to practice and preserve one's faith. The nation's diverse religious landscape fosters an atmosphere of mutual respect and coexistence among its people. Festivals from different religious traditions are celebrated with enthusiasm and participation by individuals from all faiths.

Interfaith Interactions:

Interfaith interactions are common in Nepal, reflecting the harmonious coexistence of different religious communities. Many temples and shrines are open to individuals of all faiths, promoting a sense of unity and shared spirituality. It's not uncommon to see Hindus participating in Buddhist rituals or vice versa, exemplifying the interwoven nature of religious life in Nepal.

Festivals:

Religious festivals are a highlight of Nepal's cultural calendar. Dashain, the major Hindu festival, and Tihar, the festival of lights, are celebrated with equal enthusiasm by people of all faiths. Likewise, Buddhists, Hindus, and indigenous communities participate in each other's festivals, emphasizing the nation's cultural diversity and unity.

Challenges and Resilience:

Nepal has faced its share of challenges, including political unrest and natural disasters, but its religious tolerance remains unwavering. In times of crisis, religious institutions often play a pivotal role in providing support and solace to affected communities.

In a world marked by religious strife and intolerance, Nepal stands as a shining example of religious diversity and tolerance. The nation's commitment to preserving its rich tapestry of religious traditions while fostering a spirit of unity is a testament to the resilience of its people and the enduring value of religious harmony in a multicultural society.

The Nepali Language: A Glimpse into Linguistic Diversity

In the heart of Nepal's cultural mosaic lies its diverse linguistic landscape, a testament to the nation's rich heritage and the coexistence of a multitude of languages. The Nepali language, known locally as "Nepali," serves as the lingua franca and the official language of Nepal, but this nation of stunning landscapes and cultural diversity is also home to a fascinating array of other languages.

Nepali (Nepal Bhasa):

Nepali, an Indo-Aryan language, is the most widely spoken language in Nepal, used in administration, education, and daily communication. It originated from the Khas language and was later influenced by Sanskrit, Tibetan, and other languages. The Nepali script, known as Devanagari, is used for writing. While Kathmandu Valley Newars primarily use Nepal Bhasa, most other communities use Nepali as their primary language.

Ethnic and Indigenous Languages:

Nepal's linguistic diversity is a reflection of its ethnic mosaic. More than 120 languages and dialects are spoken across the country, showcasing the vibrant tapestry of indigenous cultures. Among these languages are Maithili, Bhojpuri, Awadhi, and Magar, each with its own unique script and vocabulary.

Tibetan Influence:

In the northern regions bordering Tibet, Tibetan languages such as Sherpa, Tamang, and Tibetan itself are spoken. These languages have Tibetan scripts and are an essential part of the culture of the Himalayan communities in Nepal. The Sherpa community, in particular, is known for their role as guides and mountaineers in the Everest region.

Linguistic Diversity in the Terai:

The southern Terai plains are home to languages like Bhojpuri, Maithili, and Tharu, influenced by the languages of neighboring India. These languages have their own scripts and are reflective of the close cultural ties between Nepal and India.

Preservation and Promotion:

Efforts are underway to preserve and promote Nepal's linguistic diversity. The government recognizes several languages as national languages and promotes their use in education and administration. Additionally, cultural and linguistic preservation initiatives, including documentation and language revitalization programs, are in place to ensure the survival of these unique linguistic heritages.

Language and Identity:

Language is more than a means of communication; it's deeply intertwined with identity and culture. Many ethnic communities in Nepal take immense pride in preserving their native languages, as they serve as a powerful link to their heritage and ancestors.

Multilingualism in Everyday Life:

Nepal's linguistic diversity is not a barrier to communication but rather a testament to the nation's adaptability. It's common for Nepalis to be multilingual, proficient in both Nepali and their native languages. This linguistic versatility reflects the inclusive and harmonious nature of Nepali society.

In the tapestry of Nepal's linguistic diversity, each language is like a thread contributing to the overall richness of the nation's cultural fabric. While Nepali serves as the unifying language, the linguistic diversity of Nepal is a testament to the nation's respect for its indigenous cultures and its commitment to preserving the unique languages that make up this fascinating linguistic mosaic.

The Nepali Language: A Glimpse into Linguistic Diversity

In the heart of Nepal's cultural mosaic lies its diverse linguistic landscape, a testament to the nation's rich heritage and the coexistence of a multitude of languages. The Nepali language, known locally as "Nepali" or "Nepal Bhasa," serves as the lingua franca and the official language of Nepal, but this nation of stunning landscapes and cultural diversity is also home to a fascinating array of other languages.

Nepali, an Indo-Aryan language, is the most widely spoken language in Nepal, used in administration, education, and daily communication. It originated from the Khas language and was later influenced by Sanskrit, Tibetan, and other languages. The Nepali script, known as Devanagari, is used for writing. While Kathmandu Valley Newars primarily use Nepal Bhasa, most other communities use Nepali as their primary language.

Nepal's linguistic diversity is a reflection of its ethnic mosaic. More than 120 languages and dialects are spoken across the country, showcasing the vibrant tapestry of indigenous cultures. Among these languages are Maithili, Bhojpuri, Awadhi, and Magar, each with its own unique script and vocabulary. In the northern regions bordering Tibet, Tibetan languages such as Sherpa, Tamang, and Tibetan itself are spoken. These languages have Tibetan scripts and are an essential part of the culture of the Himalayan communities in Nepal. The Sherpa community, in particular, is known for their role as guides and mountaineers in the Everest region. The southern Terai plains are home to languages like Bhojpuri, Maithili, and Tharu, influenced by the languages of neighboring India. These languages have their own scripts and are reflective of the close cultural ties between Nepal and India.

Efforts are underway to preserve and promote Nepal's linguistic diversity. The government recognizes several languages as national languages and promotes their use in education and administration. Additionally, cultural and linguistic preservation initiatives, including documentation and language revitalization programs, are in place to ensure the survival of these unique linguistic heritages.

Language is more than a means of communication; it's deeply intertwined with identity and culture. Many ethnic communities in Nepal take immense pride in preserving their native languages, as they serve as a powerful link to their heritage and ancestors.

Nepal's linguistic diversity is not a barrier to communication but rather a testament to the nation's adaptability. It's common for Nepalis to be multilingual, proficient in both Nepali and their native languages. This linguistic versatility reflects the inclusive and harmonious nature of Nepali society.

In the tapestry of Nepal's linguistic diversity, each language is like a thread contributing to the overall richness of the nation's cultural fabric. While Nepali serves as the unifying language, the linguistic diversity of Nepal is a testament to the nation's respect for its indigenous cultures and its commitment to preserving the unique languages that make up this fascinating linguistic mosaic.

Writing Systems of Nepal: Devanagari and More

In the diverse linguistic landscape of Nepal, writing systems play a pivotal role in preserving and expressing the rich tapestry of languages spoken across the country. While Devanagari script is the most widely recognized and used writing system in Nepal, several others are equally important in capturing the nuances and complexities of the diverse languages found here.

Devanagari Script:

Devanagari, a script of Indo-Aryan origin, is the writing system primarily associated with the Nepali language. It's characterized by its flowing, cursive style and is used for writing not only Nepali but also Sanskrit and other Indo-Aryan languages. The script consists of 46 basic characters, each representing a specific sound, and is written from left to right. Devanagari is also the official script of the government of Nepal.

Nepal Bhasa Script:

Nepal Bhasa, also known as Newari, is an indigenous language spoken by the Newar community primarily in the Kathmandu Valley. The script used for Nepal Bhasa is known as Ranjana script. It's an ancient script characterized by its artistic and decorative style. Ranjana script is used for religious texts, inscriptions, and traditional art forms in Nepal Bhasa culture.

Tibetan Script:

In the northern regions of Nepal, particularly in areas bordering Tibet, Tibetan script is used for writing languages like Sherpa, Tamang, and Tibetan itself. Tibetan script is an essential part of the culture and spirituality of these Himalayan communities. It is notable for its unique and intricate characters.

Other Scripts:

Nepal's linguistic diversity extends beyond these writing systems. In the Terai region, languages like Maithili, Bhojpuri, and Tharu use scripts influenced by the Devanagari script. These scripts are adapted to suit the phonetics of the respective languages.

Promotion and Preservation:

Efforts are ongoing to promote and preserve these diverse writing systems in Nepal. The government recognizes the importance of linguistic diversity and supports initiatives aimed at script preservation, documentation, and education.

Multilingualism and Adaptability:

Nepal's linguistic diversity and the various writing systems in use are not barriers to communication but rather a testament to the adaptability of its people. It's common for individuals in Nepal to be proficient in multiple scripts and languages, reflecting the nation's commitment to inclusive and harmonious coexistence.

In the world of scripts and languages, Nepal showcases a remarkable example of how different writing systems can coexist, each contributing to the preservation of cultural identities and the expression of unique linguistic heritages. From the elegant curves of Devanagari to the artistic strokes of Ranjana and the intricate characters of Tibetan script, Nepal's writing systems are a testament to the nation's commitment to linguistic diversity and cultural richness.

The Nepali Alphabet: Vowels and Consonants

The Nepali alphabet is the key to unlocking the beauty of the Nepali language. Comprising a combination of vowels and consonants, it forms the foundation upon which the language is built. Understanding the structure of the Nepali alphabet is essential for anyone looking to delve into this rich linguistic tapestry.

Consonants:

The Nepali alphabet consists of a total of 36 consonants. Each consonant represents a unique sound and is written as an independent character. Some of the common consonants include:

1. क (ka)
2. ख (kha)
3. ग (ga)
4. घ (gha)
5. च (cha)
6. छ (chha)
7. ज (ja)
8. झ (jha)
9. ट (ṭa)
10. ठ (ṭha)
11. ड (ḍa)
12. ढ (ḍha)
13. ण (ṇa)
14. त (ta)
15. थ (tha)

16. द (da)
17. ध (dha)
18. न (na)
19. प (pa)
20. फ (pha)
21. ब (ba)
22. भ (bha)
23. म (ma)
24. य (ya)
25. र (ra)
26. ल (la)
27. व (wa)
28. श (sha)
29. ष (ṣa)
30. स (sa)
31. ह (ha)
32. ☐☐☐ (kṣa)
33. ☐☐☐ (tra)
34. ☐☐☐ (jña)
35. ञ (ña)
36. ङ (ṅa)

These consonants are the building blocks of the Nepali language, forming the skeleton of words and sentences.

Vowels:

In addition to consonants, Nepali also features a set of vowel characters. These vowels are essential for determining the pronunciation of words. Some of the common vowels include:

1. अ (a)
2. आ (ā)
3. इ (i)

4. ई (ī)
5. उ (u)
6. ऊ (ū)
7. ए (e)
8. ऐ (ai)
9. ओ (o)
10. औ (au)

Nepali vowels can be standalone characters or can be combined with consonants to create different sounds. For example, when the vowel "अ" (a) combines with the consonant "क" (ka), it becomes "□□" (kaa), representing a different sound than just "क" (ka).

Complex Characters:

Nepali also features complex characters, where a consonant and a vowel are combined into a single character. These characters are used for specific sounds that aren't represented by standalone consonants or vowels. For example, "□□" (ki) combines the consonant "क" (ka) with the vowel "इ " (i) to create a unique sound.

Understanding the Nepali alphabet and its combination of vowels and consonants is crucial for mastering the language. It forms the basis for reading, writing, and speaking Nepali fluently. Whether you're a language enthusiast, traveler, or someone looking to connect with the culture and people of Nepal, delving into the Nepali alphabet is a fascinating journey into the heart of this vibrant language.

Learning Nepali: Basic Phrases and Expressions

Learning Nepali, the heartwarming language of Nepal, opens doors to deeper cultural experiences and meaningful interactions with the friendly people of this diverse nation. While mastering a new language is a journey that takes time and practice, starting with some basic phrases and expressions can be a rewarding first step.

Greetings and Politeness:

1. **Namaste** - The universally recognized Nepali greeting. It means "I salute the divine in you." Use it with a slight bow and folded palms when meeting someone.
2. **Dhanyabad** - Thank you.
3. **Kripaya** - Please.
4. **Ramro cha** - How are you?
5. **Mitho** - Good.
6. **Maaph garnuhos** - Excuse me.
7. **Mero naam ____ ho** - My name is ____.

Common Phrases:

8. **Ke cha?** - What is it?
9. **Yahaan kahaan chha?** - Where is this?
10. **Kati samaya lagchha?** - How long will it take?
11. **Mero lagi yahaan ek chiyau dinuhos.** - Can I have a cup of tea, please?
12. **Kati paisa ho?** - How much does it cost?
13. **Ma bujchu** - I understand.

14. **Maile bujhina** - I don't understand.

Getting Around:

15. **Bus stop kahaan chha?** - Where is the bus stop?
16. **Tyo bato kata jaancha?** - Where does that road go?
17. **Yahaan sehermaan ____ kati door chha?** - How far is ____ from here?
18. **Ma aaphno hotel khojdai chu.** - I am looking for my hotel.
19. **Ma yahaan banduk kasari paainchhu?** - How do I get a taxi here?

Shopping and Eating Out:

20. **Yahaan kina khojdaichhu** - Why am I looking for it here?
21. **Yas maanche le ke garirako chha?** - What did this person order?
22. **Yas tasbir ko kimat kati ho?** - How much is the price of this picture?
23. **Ek chowk, kati ho?** - One plate, please.
24. **Kina naheriheri dinuhos?** - Why don't you give a discount?

Emergencies:

25. **Madad gara!** - Help!
26. **Aagantukko surakshya paari chha?** - Is there a tourist police here?
27. **Yahaan Hakim kahaan chha?** - Where is the doctor?
28. **Yas ko bibaadh ko laagi police bulayeko chha.** - The police have been called for this accident.

Learning these basic Nepali phrases can enhance your travel experience and foster connections with the warm-hearted people you meet along the way. Remember, the effort you put into learning and speaking the local language is often met with smiles and appreciation, making your journey through Nepal even more enjoyable. So, go ahead, embrace the language, and immerse yourself in the beauty of Nepal and its culture.

Nepali Etiquette and Customs

Understanding and respecting the customs and etiquette of Nepal is essential for travelers looking to engage deeply with the culture and build positive connections with the locals. Nepali customs and manners are rooted in tradition, hospitality, and respect for others. Here are some important aspects of Nepali etiquette to keep in mind:

1. Greetings and Respect:

- The traditional Nepali greeting is "Namaste," accompanied by a slight bow and folded hands. It signifies respect and acknowledges the divine in the other person.
- Always use the right hand or both hands when giving or receiving something, as the left hand is considered impolite.
- When entering someone's home or a temple, remove your shoes and show respect by not pointing your feet towards religious objects or people.

2. Dress Code:

- Dress modestly, especially when visiting religious sites. It's customary to cover your shoulders and knees.
- In rural areas, avoid wearing revealing clothing as it may be considered disrespectful.

3. Public Behavior:

- Public displays of affection are generally frowned upon. It's best to keep physical contact, including holding hands, to a minimum in public.
- Loud talking or shouting is considered impolite, so maintain a calm and respectful demeanor.

4. Gift-Giving:

- Bringing a small gift when visiting someone's home is a sign of appreciation. Fruits, sweets, or flowers are common choices.
- When presenting a gift, use your right hand or both hands, and receive gifts with both hands.

5. Eating Etiquette:

- When offered food or drink, it's polite to accept it, even if you don't intend to consume much.
- Use your right hand for eating, as the left hand is considered unclean. Wash your hands before and after meals.
- It's customary to wait for the host to start the meal and to express appreciation for the food.

6. Respect for Elders:

- Show respect for elders by standing when they enter the room and addressing them with appropriate honorifics, such as "dai" for older brother and "didi" for older sister.

7. Photography:

- Always ask for permission before taking photos of people, especially in rural areas. Many Nepalis are happy to oblige if you ask respectfully.

8. Religious Respect:

- When visiting temples or monasteries, follow the rules and remove your shoes before entering.
- Don't touch religious objects or idols without permission.
- Avoid walking in front of people who are praying or performing religious rituals.

9. Tipping:

- Tipping is not mandatory, but it's appreciated in the service industry. In restaurants, leaving a small tip is customary.

10. Bargaining: - Bargaining is common in markets and small shops. However, do it respectfully and with a smile.

By adhering to these customs and showing respect for Nepali traditions, you'll not only have a more enriching travel experience but also foster positive connections with the warm and welcoming people of Nepal. Embracing local etiquette is a beautiful way to engage with the culture and build meaningful relationships during your journey through this diverse and captivating country.

Handicrafts and Souvenirs: Bringing Nepal Home

Exploring Nepal's rich tapestry of handicrafts and souvenirs is an enticing journey into the heart of its artistic heritage. As you traverse this captivating country, you'll find an array of unique and beautifully crafted items that offer a piece of Nepal to take home with you. Here's a glimpse into the world of Nepali handicrafts and souvenirs:

1. Pashmina Shawls: The soft and luxurious Pashmina shawls are renowned worldwide. Handwoven from the wool of Himalayan goats, these shawls are warm, lightweight, and come in a stunning array of colors and designs.

2. Thangka Paintings: Thangka paintings are intricate Tibetan Buddhist artworks. These scroll paintings typically depict deities, mandalas, and scenes from Buddhist mythology. They make for exquisite wall decorations.

3. Handmade Paper Products: Nepal is known for its handmade Lokta paper, crafted from the bark of the Lokta plant. You can find journals, stationery, and even lampshades made from this unique paper.

4. Woodcarvings: Skilled artisans in Nepal create intricate wooden carvings, including doors, windows, and statues. These pieces often feature traditional designs and symbols.

5. Metalwork: Brass and copper items such as statues, incense burners, and singing bowls are crafted with precision and artistic flair. The resonant sound of a singing bowl is believed to have therapeutic qualities.

6. Prayer Flags: Colorful prayer flags, known as "lungta" in Tibetan, are a common sight throughout Nepal. These flags, imprinted with prayers and mantras, are hung outdoors to send blessings to the wind.

7. Jewelry: Nepali jewelry is diverse, ranging from silver and turquoise to intricate beads and gemstones. Each piece often carries cultural significance and symbolism.

8. Pottery and Ceramics: Local pottery and ceramics, including tea sets and decorative items, showcase the artistic talents of Nepali potters. They make for both functional and decorative souvenirs.

9. Singing Bowls: These handcrafted bowls produce a melodic and calming sound when struck. They are used in meditation and sound therapy and can be a unique addition to your home.

10. Masks: Traditional masks used in Nepali dances and festivals are intricate and colorful. They often depict deities, demons, or animals and can be a fascinating addition to your collection.

11. Carpets and Rugs: Hand-knotted carpets and rugs from Nepal are known for their quality and intricate designs. They are available in various sizes and patterns.

12. Textiles: You can find a wide range of textiles, including Dhaka fabric, saris, and garments made from traditional Nepali textiles. These fabrics often feature intricate patterns and vibrant colors.

When shopping for handicrafts and souvenirs in Nepal, it's essential to support local artisans and buy from reputable sources. Keep in mind that bargaining is a common practice in markets and small shops, so feel free to negotiate politely. By bringing a piece of Nepal's artistic heritage home with you, you not only acquire a beautiful keepsake but also support the talented craftsmen and women who keep these traditions alive.

The Influence of Tibetan Culture in Nepal

Nepal, nestled in the lap of the Himalayas, shares not only its geographical proximity with Tibet but also a deep and intertwined cultural heritage. The influence of Tibetan culture in Nepal is a rich and captivating aspect of the nation's identity.

Buddhism: One of the most significant cultural connections between Tibet and Nepal is Buddhism. Both countries are deeply rooted in the Buddhist tradition, and this shared faith has left an indelible mark on Nepal. Tibetan Buddhism, with its distinctive practices and rituals, has found a home in several regions of Nepal, particularly in the northern areas bordering Tibet. Monasteries and stupas built in the Tibetan style dot the landscape, offering spiritual sanctuaries and adding to the cultural tapestry of Nepal.

Tibetan Exiles: After the Chinese annexation of Tibet in the 1950s, a significant number of Tibetan refugees fled to neighboring countries, including Nepal. These Tibetan exiles brought with them their culture, religion, and traditions. The Tibetan refugee communities in Nepal, particularly in areas like Boudhanath and Swayambhunath in Kathmandu, have become centers for preserving Tibetan culture. Visitors can explore Tibetan handicrafts, art, and enjoy traditional Tibetan cuisine in these areas.

Thangka Art: Nepal is renowned for its Thangka paintings, which are central to Tibetan Buddhism. These intricate, colorful artworks often depict deities, mandalas, and spiritual scenes. Thangka painting is not only an art form but also a spiritual practice, and it thrives in Nepal, showcasing the deep influence of Tibetan culture.

Language and Scripts: Tibetan script, closely related to the Devanagari script used in Nepal, is still used in some religious texts and inscriptions. The influence of Tibetan script and language in Nepal's cultural landscape is a testament to the enduring connection between the two regions.

Religious Festivals: Nepal hosts numerous festivals influenced by Tibetan culture. Losar, the Tibetan New Year, is celebrated with fervor in Tibetan communities across Nepal. During this time, vibrant processions, dance performances, and religious rituals take place, offering visitors a glimpse into the rich traditions of Tibet.

Cuisine: Tibetan cuisine has also made its mark in Nepal. Dishes like momo (dumplings), thukpa (noodle soup), and yak-based products are popular in Tibetan-influenced regions. These culinary delights add a unique flavor to Nepal's diverse gastronomy.

Cultural Exchange: Cultural exchange between Nepal and Tibet has been ongoing for centuries. Pilgrims, scholars, and traders have traversed the mountainous terrain, exchanging ideas, art, and spirituality. This exchange continues today, as travelers from around the world visit Nepal to explore the shared heritage of these two regions.

The influence of Tibetan culture in Nepal is a testament to the enduring connections forged by geography, history, and spirituality. It adds a layer of diversity and richness to Nepal's cultural mosaic, making it a fascinating destination for those seeking to delve into the intersection of two ancient and profound traditions.

The Gurkhas: Nepal's Brave Warriors

The Gurkhas, often referred to as Nepal's Brave Warriors, are a legendary force with a history steeped in valor, loyalty, and unmatched military prowess. These extraordinary soldiers have earned their reputation on battlefields across the globe, and their story is one of unwavering dedication and bravery.

Origins and Early History: The origins of the Gurkhas can be traced back to the mid-18th century when King Prithvi Narayan Shah of Gorkha unified the small kingdoms and principalities of Nepal into a single nation. The word "Gurkha" is derived from the name of the town Gorkha. It was during this time that these soldiers came to be known for their exceptional martial skills and loyalty.

Serving the British Crown: The Gurkhas first came to the attention of the British East India Company during the Anglo-Nepalese War (1814-1816). Impressed by their bravery, the British signed the Treaty of Sugauli in 1815, which allowed them to recruit Gurkhas into their military ranks. This marked the beginning of a longstanding association between the Gurkhas and the British Army.

World Wars and Beyond: Gurkha regiments played crucial roles in both World War I and World War II. Their fearlessness and determination on the battlefield earned them numerous honors and decorations. The motto of the Gurkhas, "Better to die than be a coward," encapsulates their unwavering commitment.

Modern Gurkhas: Today, Gurkha soldiers continue to serve in the British Army, the Indian Army, and the Gurkha Contingent of the Singapore Police Force. They are renowned for their proficiency in various military skills, including close combat, marksmanship, and jungle warfare.

Gurkha Values: One of the defining characteristics of Gurkha soldiers is their unswerving loyalty. The bond between a Gurkha and their British or Indian officer, known as a "sahib," is often described as akin to that of family. This loyalty, combined with their exceptional skills, has made them a respected and cherished part of the armed forces in the countries they serve.

Legacy and Recognition: Gurkhas have received numerous awards for their gallantry in battle, including the Victoria Cross, the highest military decoration in the British Empire. Their legacy is celebrated in various ways, from monuments and museums to events like the Gurkha Cup, a football tournament held annually.

The Gurkhas' remarkable history is a testament to the indomitable spirit and courage of the Nepali people. Their unwavering dedication to duty and their reputation as fearsome warriors have left an indelible mark on the annals of military history, and they continue to be a source of pride for Nepal and the nations they serve. The story of the Gurkhas is one of bravery, honor, and a profound commitment to defending the principles they hold dear.

The 2015 Earthquake and Nepal's Resilience

The year 2015 was a pivotal and heartbreaking moment in Nepal's history. On April 25th of that year, a catastrophic earthquake, with a magnitude of 7.8, struck the heart of the nation. It was a seismic event that shook not only the earth beneath Nepal but also the very core of its society, culture, and resilience.

The Tremors and Destruction: The earthquake's epicenter was in Gorkha district, just west of the capital, Kathmandu. The initial shockwaves and subsequent aftershocks wreaked havoc, causing extensive damage to buildings, infrastructure, and historical landmarks. Centuries-old temples, palaces, and homes were reduced to rubble in a matter of seconds.

Human Toll: The human toll was devastating. Thousands lost their lives, and many more were injured or left homeless. The earthquake's impact rippled across the country, affecting rural and remote areas, where access to aid and relief was often challenging.

International Response: The earthquake triggered a massive international response. Countries from around the world, humanitarian organizations, and individuals rallied to provide support, relief, and aid to Nepal. This outpouring of solidarity was heartening in the face of such immense tragedy.

Nepal's Resilience: Nepal's response to the earthquake was characterized by its resilience. Despite the overwhelming destruction and loss, the people of Nepal came together to support one another. Communities united to provide shelter, food, and comfort to those in need. The spirit of "help thy neighbor" was a shining beacon of hope amid the darkness.

Rebuilding and Recovery: The task of rebuilding was monumental. Nepal's government, with assistance from the international community, embarked on a long and arduous journey to reconstruct the nation. This involved not only physically rebuilding infrastructure but also addressing the emotional and psychological scars left by the earthquake.

Lessons Learned: The earthquake of 2015 served as a stark reminder of Nepal's vulnerability to seismic activity. It also highlighted the importance of disaster preparedness and resilience. In the years that followed, efforts were made to strengthen building codes, improve early warning systems, and enhance disaster response capabilities.

A Continuing Journey: As time has passed, Nepal has made significant strides in its recovery and reconstruction efforts. While the scars of the earthquake remain, they serve as a testament to the strength and determination of the Nepali people. The nation has emerged from the rubble with a renewed commitment to building a safer, more resilient future.

The earthquake of 2015 will forever be etched in Nepal's history, not only for the devastation it caused but for the resilience and strength it brought to the forefront. It is a testament to the human spirit's ability to endure, adapt, and rebuild in the face of unimaginable challenges. Nepal's journey from disaster to recovery is a story of hope, unity, and unwavering determination.

Nepal's Economic Landscape: Challenges and Opportunities

Nepal's economic landscape is a complex terrain marked by both challenges and opportunities. As a landlocked country nestled amidst the towering Himalayas, Nepal faces unique economic dynamics that shape its development trajectory.

Agriculture as the Backbone: A significant portion of Nepal's population relies on agriculture for their livelihood. Subsistence farming is prevalent, with crops like rice, wheat, maize, and millet being staples. The agricultural sector contributes substantially to the country's GDP and employs a significant portion of the workforce.

Challenges in Agriculture: Despite its importance, Nepal's agricultural sector faces challenges such as limited access to modern farming techniques, inadequate irrigation facilities, and vulnerability to climate change. These factors can impact food security and livelihoods, making it essential to invest in agricultural development.

Hydropower Potential: Nepal boasts significant hydropower potential, thanks to its abundant rivers and water resources. Exploiting this potential not only addresses the country's energy needs but also offers opportunities for revenue generation through export to neighboring countries.

Infrastructure Development: Nepal's infrastructure, including roads and transportation networks, is in various stages of development. The mountainous terrain presents engineering challenges, but improved infrastructure connectivity can enhance trade and economic growth.

Tourism as a Key Sector: Nepal's stunning natural beauty and cultural heritage make it a magnet for tourists and trekkers. Tourism plays a pivotal role in the economy, contributing substantially to foreign exchange earnings and providing employment opportunities.

Challenges in Tourism: While tourism is a vital sector, it faces challenges like infrastructure deficiencies, seasonal fluctuations, and the need for sustainable practices to preserve Nepal's pristine environment.

Trade Relations: Nepal maintains trade relations with neighboring countries, primarily India and China. Trade agreements and transit routes are crucial for the country's economic stability and access to international markets.

Remittances: A significant portion of Nepal's population works abroad, particularly in the Gulf countries and Malaysia, sending remittances back home. Remittances play a crucial role in improving living standards and supporting local economies.

Economic Challenges: Nepal faces economic challenges, including a high poverty rate, income inequality, and a reliance on remittances. Political instability has also impacted economic growth and investment.

Opportunities for Growth: Despite challenges, Nepal's economic landscape offers several opportunities. These include harnessing hydropower resources, expanding tourism, improving agricultural practices, and promoting sustainable development.

International Aid and Investment: International aid and foreign direct investment can play a significant role in Nepal's economic development. Projects in sectors like infrastructure, energy, and education are avenues for growth.

Conclusion: Nepal's economic landscape is multifaceted, reflecting the country's unique geography and social dynamics. While challenges persist, there are promising opportunities for sustainable economic growth and development. Overcoming obstacles and capitalizing on strengths will be crucial in shaping Nepal's economic future.

Sustainable Tourism in Nepal: Preserving Natural Beauty

Sustainable tourism in Nepal is a crucial aspect of both the country's economic development and the preservation of its unparalleled natural beauty. Nestled amidst the Himalayas, Nepal is a land of breathtaking landscapes, diverse flora and fauna, and rich cultural heritage. However, the influx of tourists, if not managed sustainably, can pose threats to these invaluable assets.

Economic Significance: Tourism is a cornerstone of Nepal's economy. It generates foreign exchange, provides employment opportunities, and supports local communities. The revenue from tourism contributes significantly to the nation's GDP.

Preserving Natural Beauty: One of Nepal's greatest assets is its pristine natural beauty. The towering peaks of the Himalayas, lush forests, and serene lakes attract travelers from around the world. Sustainable tourism practices are essential to protect these natural wonders for future generations.

Responsible Trekking: Trekking is a popular activity in Nepal, with visitors embarking on journeys to renowned destinations like the Everest Base Camp and Annapurna Circuit. Sustainable trekking involves responsible waste disposal, minimizing environmental impact, and respecting local cultures.

Community Involvement: Engaging local communities in tourism initiatives is vital for sustainable development. When communities benefit from tourism, they are more inclined to protect their environment and cultural heritage.

Wildlife Conservation: Nepal is home to diverse wildlife, including the Bengal tiger and one-horned rhinoceros. Sustainable tourism initiatives support wildlife conservation efforts by raising awareness and funding protection measures.

Promoting Eco-Friendly Practices: Sustainable tourism encourages eco-friendly practices, such as using renewable energy sources, reducing single-use plastics, and supporting eco-lodges that minimize their environmental footprint.

Cultural Preservation: Nepal's rich cultural heritage is a draw for tourists. Sustainable tourism involves respecting local customs and traditions while promoting cultural exchange and understanding.

Challenges and Solutions: Nepal faces challenges in achieving sustainable tourism, including infrastructure limitations, waste management issues, and potential overcrowding in popular areas. Solutions include investing in infrastructure, implementing waste management systems, and diversifying tourism offerings to reduce pressure on specific regions.

Government Initiatives: The Nepali government has taken steps to promote sustainable tourism, including establishing protected areas and implementing responsible trekking regulations.

Conclusion: Sustainable tourism in Nepal is not just a choice but a necessity. Preserving the natural beauty and cultural heritage of this remarkable nation while reaping the economic benefits of tourism requires a delicate balance. With responsible practices, community involvement, and continued efforts from all stakeholders, Nepal can ensure that its natural treasures remain unspoiled for generations to come.

Epilogue

The journey through the pages of this book, exploring the wonders and intricacies of Nepal, has been nothing short of extraordinary. We've embarked on a voyage across the diverse landscapes, delved deep into the rich tapestry of history, and marveled at the cultural vibrancy that defines this Himalayan nation. As we approach the end of our literary expedition, let's take a moment to reflect on the essence of Nepal.

Nepal is a land of contrasts, where towering peaks touch the sky, and lush valleys teem with life. It's a place where ancient traditions coexist with modern aspirations, and where spirituality infuses every aspect of daily life. Nepal is a testament to resilience, having weathered both natural and political storms, emerging stronger each time.

From the majestic mountains of the Annapurna and Everest regions to the tranquil lakes of Pokhara and Rara, from the bustling streets of Kathmandu to the serene temples of Lumbini, Nepal's diversity is its greatest asset. Its people, with their warmth and hospitality, welcome visitors with open arms, sharing their traditions, stories, and smiles.

The history of Nepal, from its early dynasties to the unification under King Prithvi Narayan Shah and its encounters with the British Raj, is a tapestry woven with valor and diplomacy. The legacy of the Buddha, born in Lumbini, continues to inspire spiritual seekers worldwide, while the vibrant festivals and rituals showcase Nepal's deep-rooted cultural heritage.

Nepal's geography, with its challenging terrain and pristine landscapes, has molded its identity, from the resilient Gurkha warriors to the enduring spirit of its people in the face of natural disasters like the 2015 earthquake.

Sustainable tourism, preserving the natural beauty while providing economic opportunities, is a path Nepal has embraced for its future. This approach ensures that generations to come can witness the splendor of the Himalayas, explore the diverse wildlife, and partake in the rich traditions.

As we conclude this journey through Nepal, let us carry with us the beauty of its landscapes, the wisdom of its history, and the warmth of its people. Nepal is not just a destination; it's an experience that leaves an indelible mark on the heart and soul. The Himalayan nation beckons, inviting you to explore its mysteries, engage with its people, and be enchanted by its beauty. Nepal, with its timeless allure, is a place where the past meets the future, and where every traveler becomes a storyteller.

Printed in Great Britain
by Amazon